EXCEPTIONAL AMERICA

God Bless America.
From Nick.

EXCEPTIONAL AMERICA

A Message of Hope from a Modern-Day de Tocqueville

NICK ADAMS

iUniverse, Inc.
Bloomington

EXCEPTIONAL AMERICA
A Message of Hope from a Modern-Day de Tocqueville

Copyright © 2012 by Nick Adams.
www.nickadamsinamerica.com

All rights reserved. No part of this book may be used or reproduced by any means, graphic, electronic, or mechanical, including photocopying, recording, taping or by any information storage retrieval system without the written permission of the publisher except in the case of brief quotations embodied in critical articles and reviews.

HE HOLY BIBLE, NEW INTERNATIONAL VERSION®, NIV® Copyright © 1973, 1978, 1984, 2011 by Biblica, Inc.™ Used by permission. All rights reserved worldwide.

iUniverse books may be ordered through booksellers or by contacting:

iUniverse
1663 Liberty Drive
Bloomington, IN 47403
www.iuniverse.com
1-800-Authors (1-800-288-4677)

Because of the dynamic nature of the Internet, any web addresses or links contained in this book may have changed since publication and may no longer be valid. The views expressed in this work are solely those of the author and do not necessarily reflect the views of the publisher, and the publisher hereby disclaims any responsibility for them.

Any people depicted in stock imagery provided by Thinkstock are models, and such images are being used for illustrative purposes only.
Certain stock imagery © Thinkstock.

ISBN: 978-1-4759-1768-0 (sc)
SBN: 978-1-4759-1818-2 (ebk)

Printed in the United States of America

iUniverse rev. date: 04/19/2012

*For my mom and dad who have always
supported me.
I love you so very much.*

TABLE OF CONTENTS

Foreword ix

Chapter 1	The Cowboy Spirit 1
Chapter 2	Old Glory 17
Chapter 3	Faith 32
Chapter 4	God's Troops 52
Chapter 5	Exceptional and Indispensable 69
Chapter 6	Mercantilism 88
Chapter 7	Character 104
Chapter 8	Constitutionally Limited Government 129
Chapter 9	Imperiled 152
Chapter 10	The Future 174
Chapter 11	The Nature of the American Boomerang 190

FOREWORD

The American nation is without peer; in the almost five thousand years of recorded human history, it is unlike any other. Irrespective of the direction the human mind pivots, whether to the past or the end of the long track of which humanity is yet to tread, the American experiment is central. Sociological appraisal of the nation is a most ambitious project, for the American ensured at his outset a transcendental existence; his is not so much a nation or geographic entity but an idea of endurance.

It therefore occasions limited surprise that such a unique construct stirs the deepest of human emotion, both within and without the American society. The idea, even more than the nation-state, is a most fertile soil for passionate human sensation and interaction. The idea, and its sequential consequences or elements, may be accompanied by any number of fierce sentiment: misgiving or inspiration; misunderstanding or appreciation; loyalty or unfaithfulness; approval or repudiation. Ambivalence may be directed at the nation but seldom at the idea. And so it is the case with the idea of America, engendering tumultuous human opinion worldwide with a diversity reminiscent of its land and demography.

Ideas are distinct to nations; they develop almost instantly a common language of citizenship and infuse a national narrative with romance, fostering the virtues of patriotism and optimism. Connected to the idea, is the value—social constants defining of the cultural composite. The nature and background of the idea are determining of all remaining characteristics.

The American belief in and of human freedom, accompanied by powerful personal and civic Christian faith, provide a robust individualism and notable libertarian streak. The idea, and the sum of its elements, combines to produce an electric synergy of exceptionalism fitting to the most individualistic, optimistic, moralistic, patriotic, and religious and libertarian nation of the world. More than this, it presents a nation with little semblance to even its closest English-speaking cultural cousins, and fundamentally opposed to the nations of Europe. Not even its fellow frontier nation and most steadfast ally, Australia, has lived up to expectations.

Envy, the most corrosive element of human nature, is expected by an omnipotent superpower such as America. But the values of the idea of America create a supplementary venom far more poisonous. The founding of America, and her principles, which still breathe life today, are profoundly antithetic to the liberal or progressive agendas advocating collectivism, relativism and greater government. The American nation, founded in anti-statist sentiment and belief in the individual, has continued to develop further its inherently conservative founding, to embody the heart of conservative thought. Put another way, conservative values such as individualism, patriotism, Christianity, limited government and support of Israel, are traditional American values. These defining values have, until recently, been mostly celebrated in the national polity and personified in the individual character. With any idea, there exists paradox and inconsistency; the American is no exception. Genuine freedom will always invite extremity and contradiction, and within this nation it resides. But it cannot be said that the exception, no matter how stark, disproves the rule.

One need only compare the ideological positions of the progressive and the conservative or the American: the left believes in a collectivist society; the American in the individual. The left subscribes to cultural relativism; the American the most patriotic of men. The left believe in more government and greater regulation; the American a man who wishes for minimalist government presence in his life. The left promote radical multiculturalism; the American *E pluribus unum*. The left is uncomfortable in the presence of superpower, and disliking of the nation-state; the American a harsh critic of the supra-national body such as the United Nations. The left are the loudest supporters of Palestine; the American a no greater friend of Israel. The left has reservations and seek to intervene in markets; the American the greatest and purest capitalist alive. Indeed, it is the cultural conservatism of the American that offends most.

The enmity of the international elites of media and academic, in this light, becomes eminently more understandable. It also explains the deep sense of despair and anger of tens of millions of Americans toward the Obama administration and its unprecedented governmental overreach. It would appear that this is the first administration of the American nation with clear sympathies for a European-based secular left model, a sharp departure from the national culture with enormous ramifications on the national psyche. This departure could not have occurred at a worse time for the American, perplexing an already limping with battered morale, injured confidence, major unemployment, a struggling economy and weak dollar.

The emptiness and relativism of the words of President Obama at the G20 Summit in the UK in the spring of 2009, struck at the soul of the proud American:

> I believe in American exceptionalism, just as I suspect that the Brits believe in British exceptionalism and the Greeks believe in Greek exceptionalism.

These words were uttered in response to a question, when asked if President Obama believes in American exceptionalism. His statement came just four weeks before I arrived for the first time to the shores of America to travel through America to study her exceptionalism, having been inspired by the great French philosopher, Alexis de Tocqueville.

Almost a hundred and eighty years ago, the twenty-six-year-old Frenchman arrived on the shores of America to travel extensively across a young nation. Five years later, he wrote about the greatness of America. This year, 2012, marks the one hundred and seventy seventh birthday of his prophetic masterpiece, entitled *Democracy in America*. During the almost two centuries since, there has been a conspicuous dearth of recorded foreign observation and analysis of the greatness of America.

De Tocqueville's book remains the only time in the history of America that a foreigner, an outsider, has written a comprehensive account of his journey through America, focusing solely on American exceptionalism. And so, the world was a starkly different place when de Tocqueville penned his masterwork, framed around his travels with his friend to America, now considered a classic of sociology and political science. While some elements are outdated, the book's substantive content is as accurate and trenchant as it was nearly two centuries ago. Sadly, his analysis has been forgotten by some, and discarded by world elites and their American counterparts. His findings were of an exceptional America, hailing various national characteristics he saw as central to this conclusion; anathematic to the cultural relativism that has gripped the Western world.

Across five trips over two years, I would spend nine months traveling in the continental United States; the exact length of de Tocqueville's famous journey. Crisscrossing the nation from west to east, north to south, visiting more than twenty states by plane, train, car, bus, and horse and cart, I observed the character and culture of a people that had captured my heart and imagination even as a young child. From small towns to big cities; deserts to forests; museums to rodeos; city lights to ranches, and; suburban homes to businesses: I felt the excitement of the heady and steady pulse of American exceptionalism.

Clearly, I arrived in America with substantial prejudice; a fascination for the nation had blossomed from childhood with the maturing of my Christian faith and time at university, developing a staunchly pro-American perspective. These matters further crystallized with the events of September 11; I remember, as a seventeen-year-old, watching wordlessly and hoping helplessly by the television as the cowardly, dastardly and positively evil acts were repeatedly replayed. I felt the distinct flush of patriotic resentment, understanding immediately that my political and worldview had been indelibly shaped. History has a capacity to bestow upon a generation a particular role; I knew then and there it was the responsibility to embrace and defend the American nation.

Accompanying this were my political convictions: a belief in God; the traditional family; personal responsibility; the sanctity of human life, patriotism, self-reliance, individual liberty; free markets; limited government; the state of Israel; a strong national defense, and; that welfare should be ideally be the role of non-government actors, particularly the church and family. I was hardly aware that these very convictions were the engine of American exceptionalism; now the reasons for my attraction to America are patently evident.

I felt impelled to embark on this project, propelled by the constant, fatuous, inane and sadly, ever-increasing anti-Americanism existing across the globe. The time for an analysis of American greatness could hardly be more poignant, with the nation facing its sternest test; the end of American power and inevitable ascent of China declared. It is essential, once more, for an outside voice to express the potential that this country has to offer human civilization. As one close American friend suggested to me: "Sometimes it takes someone on the outside to tell us or remind us what we are like on the inside." Many Americans privy to this project have indicated that it is most fitting for an Australian to have undertaken it, aware that the America has had no more intimate or steady ally since the beginning of the twentieth century. Australia is the only nation to have fought alongside America in every major conflict since the First World War.

Sadly, the American can count his true friends on one hand. But it is his relationship with his founding principles that cause far greater consternation. Let it be clear: we are not operating in a post-American world. It still stands comfortably as the greatest country of the world. But America is falling behind—not behind other nations, but behind her promise and potential. Since President Reagan, it has flirted with the economic and government ideas of Europe; its businesses and individuals more encumbered in red tape than ever before, and; its classrooms are increasingly captive to the academic elite, with many schools active in removing all references to God and Bible, and prone to imparting their own jaundiced views on the Constitution and Declaration of Independence.

Of the threats to America, none presents greater danger than a school of thought, either espoused by government or contemplated by ordinary Americans, that American exceptionalism does not exist. American exceptionalism is not an opinion or moral judgment but a testable and falsifiable hypothesis; more than that, it is a foundational cultural value of America. Any action drawing doubt to its exceptionality fundamentally changes America. The doctrine of relativism is as perilous to Western civilization as radical Islam and communism. In fact, the myopic world of relativism gives life to these grave threats. Relativism believes in everything but believes in nothing. It accords that no culture, religion, nation, or person is any more successful than or superior to any other. Perhaps the twenty-sixth President of the United States, Theodore Roosevelt put it best:

> The man who loves other countries as much as his own stands on a level with the man who loves other women as much as he loves his own wife.

The book is aimed at every American who believes in the foundational idea and values of America. It should remind the reader that despite the anti-Americanism lurking in the world and the negativity screamed on the front pages of newspapers, America is, for all her shortcomings, a fountainhead of everything we consider great or noble in mankind.

Some will suggest many of my analyses are naïve and romanticized; to them, I say I have fresh and unique eyes, and accept the advantages and disadvantages that sight carries. There is scant doubt my work will be derided as tautological and not falsifiable. As Thucydides twenty-four-hundred years ago, I offer my work, not as a politically captivating tabloid designed for instant gratification, but rather a personal testament intended for future generations.

In this book, I continuously refer to "the American." "The American" is the idealized American; by no means every American living in America. Culturally conservative with a providential worldview, "the American" is a man of family, faith, flag, and neighborhood; defined of the belief that his past achievements, future opportunities, and blessings come from his Creator, not his government. He is proudly principled, passionately individualistic, and resolutely self-determined, believing every person can rise above the circumstances of their birth and achieve any outcome. This definition clearly precludes; it is only my hope that I can help those Americans see and become such subjects. The romanticism of America is its greatest survival mechanism; to overcome its trials of today, it must once more embrace the idealism that inspires and defines; the same idealism that has me penning this book. The "outsider," to whom I also refer, does not constitute every outsider. I am a case in point.

Without sound economic management and a stable economy, the attainment of cultural conservative ends is impossible. It will be the winner of the cultural war that will determine the fate of America. A common view championed today is that the American should manage his decline gracefully; this gratuitous advice premised on an error of judgment. I believe America, in spite of her current turmoil, is only in the infancy of her greatness.

I would like to appropriately express my gratitude—though no "thank you" could be fully adequate—to all those who helped create, support, and complete this project. But the greatest thank you must be directed first and foremost to the idea and nation of America, her military, and her people. Their leadership of the world and undying friendship of freedom and democracy has inspired generations, including me. Freedom, liberty, justice, democracy, and bravery are the principles you have advocated and protected at enormous cost. I appreciate and applaud you.

God bless America.

Nick Adams
Sydney, Australia
March 2012

Chapter 1
THE COWBOY SPIRIT

It has been said by those wishing to lampoon this land that it is, even today, replete with cowboys. I cannot disagree with this assertion based on my experience but I must say that the presence of the cowboy spirit can only aid a national polity, and so it is, in the case of the American. It is true that one of the most recognizable American images in the world is the cowboy and the visitor is reminded of his spirit, one of omnipresence, many times during any given day.

Where most of the world is quick to criticize the cowboy as old-fashioned, masculine and anti-intellectual, I find the American embraces him warmly. The cowboy, when one applies reflection, is an enduring personification of American society and her values; he does not ride in groups, he has only his horse and bare necessities; he is a man of action without assistance. His horse is synonymous with freedom. Self-made, free, and self-reliant, he exudes confidence, certainty, and strength: the ultimate success. Travelling across this great land, any visitor understands the cowboy spirit may not be as alive and prevalent in America as it once was, but I must report that it is far more alive and customary here than anywhere else man inhabits. Such breath the cowboy spirit has here; its leaders rush to be associated with the qualities of the cowboy, ensuring he or she be photographed with hat on horseback. The leaders of these communities are swift to recognize the resonance of this image with the will and nature of his fellow American man, and his passion for, or preoccupation with, the individual. It is difficult to consider the cowboy persona as anything other than the natural state of man and the visitor feels that the American understands this intuitively. I, too, understand the equation: to blister the individual is to abase the founding of this nation and to adulterate nature.

Here the values of this society have become the country; a state most unsurprising and logical, but a correlation perhaps overlooked. Studying the self-made character of the American and observing his behavioral tendencies is most useful in understanding the actions of his government in the world stage. This nation bears the identifiable individualism of the American himself; it is the only individual of the world theatre, often acting alone and with ambitious vision. It should be in the minds of the many harboring sentiment against this land, defogged: where other nations want to manage; the American desires to transform, a natural appetite of the self-made man. The penchant for transformation that engulfs the American so, is unable to spring from the collectivist—a man of inherent preference for compromise and consensus without action. The national leaders of this land, in their ambitions, display the aggression and masculinity allied to the individual.

A Land of Beauty

The visitor on his maiden voyage to this great land is first struck by her sheer size and scale; his fresh eyes startled, overwhelmed by the impressive and expansive physical display of the American metropolis and broader geographical diversity. With little effort, he can instinctively imagine the feelings of the earliest Americans upon viewing the stunning vista of the unspoiled frontier, with all its arresting seduction. The sights in the human eye of the contemporary American landscape may be strikingly different to those visions reflected in the pupils of the remarkable first arrivals but both unite with their ability to move, impose and overpower man's mind. This land is one with matchless variety, beauty, energy, and life; its diversity such, the visitor may be forgiven for considering the fifty states as almost fifty varying countries.

It matters minimally in which exact geographical location of the expanse you may find yourself; be it the Iowan cornfields, the rolling farmland of Ohio, the prairies of Illinois, the river banks of Missouri or the glaciers of Montana, the distinctive diversity of American nature mirrors the unique properties of the landscape of the American culture. With more than three hundred million people living in a continental landmass stretching over some three thousand miles, this country achieves the implausible: the fusing of diversity and uniformity, separating herself from all other nations. These matters alone lead to an inescapable conclusion; even the twenty-first-century visitor cannot depart from the substantive assessments of the early visitors of foreign lands of preceding centuries. I cannot faithfully assert otherwise: this nation and its people are profoundly different to any other, in both qualitative and quantitive measurement. The most cursory of engagement and briefest of stays is required to reach this analysis in this land; the exceptional matters of the character of the American citizen and his polity are unsubtle, if not vivid.

To the external source, the enormous paradox of the American is that he is a man imbued with equal doses of extreme individualism and unified nationalism; a prescription exclusive to the American drugstore. These enduring, exceptional circumstances that still awe the visitor today wear the designs of the American founders; men intent on stenciling onto the mental sheets and historical pages of incoming generations the difference between this land and other nations. The repudiation of an overbearing central government, state religion or parliamentary system to achieve this end remains to the observer highly visible in the composition of the American identity. The American is most praiseful of his founders, speaking in the reverential tones usually reserved for the famous member of the family, extending them great favor in both private and public forums. Such acclamation yields little surprise; the wild and unprecedented success of this experiment is prevailingly due to these magnificent and prescient men. It must be said that as one traverses this land in any direction, the palpable feeling remains that this is a nation governed by the people. The citizen of this land is quick to remind you that his founders were highly suspicious of democracy; a republic favored, that was to be a government of laws, not men. But this is hardly where the exceptionalism stops; these circumstances were not sufficient for the American, discontented with the mere equality of each individual vote, bruised by his past encounters. He insisted, and in large part, still insists today, that the rights of every one of his number be protected from an overly powerful central government. As I watch the American recount his foundations, I realize it impossible to conceive of a man with greater ineradicable and indwelling passion for his sovereignty, and that of his fellow man. He celebrates it with volume and vibrancy; it is his individual sovereignty that mints and orientates his culture and community, not the government.

But these are the physical matters of the political; it is the visceral matters of the cultural that stem from the seeds of this founding that truly excite and differentiate. It is the values of this nation that serve as the bone and sinew of the American life, I have concluded. The value is the social constant that determines, transforms, and transcends its society, delivering the virtue of optimism and the comfort of certainty, among countless others. But the value is a most precious and fragile substance; the absence of care, courage or dedication dilutes, erodes, or ignores it. The immediate corollaries of the polity deficient in courage are the contaminants of ambiguity, instability and self-doubt.

The foreign visit to this grand land reveals an instinctively culturally conservative and optimistic society, a stark contrast to the state of all Western nations, occupants of an age referred to by Catholic Pope Joseph Ratzinger, as one of "agnosticism, of relativism, of disenchantment, of presumption." As my footprints increase in number on this soil rich in values, I confront the reality that this terrain is only relatively unaffected by the drought of political correctness and permissiveness. The American is possibly the only man on this earth who does not wrestle with his identity. He knows, without the slightest hint of doubt, who he is.

A Man of Principle

The visitor finds that the American holds dear his values with folded arms as if clasping a crook; they are robust and unyielding and today only increasing in utility. This moral ecology separates the American from his peers, perpetuating the exceptionalism of his founding and experience. A man of principle is an extraordinary man; it is in this context that the visitor quickly grasps the super success of this nation; a nation without peer. The traditions of this nation define its culture; it is a culture that does not cast the individual to conformity with set customs, rather it is a culture that fosters the individual and his character, leaving any outsider convinced of the exceptional nature of the tradition of independence.

Individual freedom, political liberty, justice, republican democracy, and bravery are matters of the American heart; principles that form the beat of its mighty pulse. It would seem of the American experience that enduring founding principles translate to lasting values. In fact, it must be said no sphere exists that is dominated by the American that is not underpinned by these distinctive ideals; it is also the explanation of any seemingly unusual or idiosyncratic feature of American life. The powerful Christianity, muscular patriotism, or ubiquity of the military, three defining characteristics of the polity here, are enmeshed with the values set found in the American household. Most impressively, the outsider further finds that the American genuinely asserts and believes that his values afford him moral and cultural superiority; a viewpoint hardly disputatious even to the most hardened and colored of observers.

I find the American to be most forthright and proficient at all times in his speaking, but particularly in an exposition of his values; he prompts frequently that there is little purpose to possessing enduring values, unless they are celebrated and actively pursued. It is refreshing to hear the honesty and enthusiasm of the principled tongue; he speaks sense: being afraid to speak your values is as good as possessing none.

But it is within these same impressive exchanges that one quickly identifies the source of the indisposition of many citizens of other lands toward the American. He is a man that raises the international ire of those highly sensitized and meek populations, conditioned to loathe such confidence and volume, particularly on a subject for which their shortcomings are notable. His simplistic and uncompromising convictions bring enormous discomfort to the men of societies where the visceral is traduced from birth. The American struggles to comprehend the English-speaking man of another land hailing from a nation that extends to him similar liberties, yet he expends little energy or cultural intensity to celebrate their existence.

This is simultaneously the great demarcation and controversy of this land; the man with strong values is an automatic candidate for, and subject of, envy and loathing. It is quickly realized once here that it is cultural distinction at the origin of the anti-American disease. It takes a man of only limited intellect to discern that the innate insistence of the defense of freedom at any price espoused by the American is greatly incongruous to the apathetic nonchalance of his Western cousins. The polity is here is markedly different to those of the other lands; there is no virtue seen in conformity, and nor is it fostered by culture. To favor silence, even in disagreement, a most common trait in the men of other cultures, is considered here the zenith of weakness. I have discerned here that it is the case that man is instructed from an early age to characterize submission that is unaccompanied by struggle, as shameful. Within the conformist society and its praise for those that quietly participate, it is clear the manner, style, and views of the American would be perceived as intemperate and irritable.

I find that the American is a man most undisposed to nuance; he fervently believes in the concepts of righteousness and wickedness. His proclivity for the absolute leaves him wide open to the charge of hypocrisy but he seems unbothered, remaining blithe. He is a man overflowing in optimism; even during the Civil War and his early defeats by the British, predictions of the dominion shifting from the other side of the Atlantic were routine.

Celebrated Individualism

The uniformity of individualism ranges from the detectable to the conspicuous. It matters in this country not in the least where one visits; man strives to distinguish himself with distinction. From the gospel music, mint juleps, and sultry belles of the South to the snowy wastes of Minnesota to the spectacular canyons of Nevada, this land is different to all other nations in important ways; it is with these variances that the American seems to have endowed himself with unique characteristics, causing it to follow exceptional paths. The visitor feels the physicality of individualism of the country; it clearly is the foundational difference for this land. In the presence of this fierce individuality, it is as if all dullness flees, and man is once more animated, far away from the inertness of the foreign society.

It would appear that the individuality that immerses the culture and psyche of this society is the heritage of the early Calvinist settlers; the men and women espousing the utmost importance of the individual and his direct relationship with God. From interaction with the American of today, the visitor effortlessly deduces that these are the descendants of the highly individualistic and untypical Europeans with aspiration that sought desperately the soil of economic opportunity. Self-reliance, independence and exceptionalism, the themes of Calvinist thought, quite clearly remain the defining attributes of the American experience; values the Calvinists spread with great speed from the Eastern frontier westward.

I feel that it must be said: individualism is one of the lost virtues of our time, lying at the heart of the civil society. It cannot be denied that the impenetrable fence guarding from socialistic intrusion and its violent home invasion with its brutally middling effect is the magnificent principle of individualism. It is true, and the American is most cognizant of it: groupthink produces mediocrity and drudgery. Individuality is indeed the driver of innovation and creativity.

The person living in an individualistic society is less likely to believe he is entitled automatically to a share of anything, is less troubled by inequality, and is driven to provide for himself and his family through his own effort, and so it is most certainly here with the American. He expects little and believes all to be possible. Influencing virtually every aspect of his culture and central to the possibility and existence of the American dream, it is along with Christianity, the explanation of extraordinary American accomplishment, one must conclude. He most patently believes and is wedded to the inspirational ideology that he has morphed into maxim: any man can rise above the circumstances of his birth and achieve anything he strives to achieve. There appears to be, with only the notable exception of the man in this country who describes himself as a liberal, that there is hardly a citizen anywhere here who views individual success as contingent on government or union support. There is, according to the grand American view, no class of people forever condemned to poverty or guaranteed wealth.

The reading of his famed Declaration of Independence and the Constitution by the outsider have for centuries now revealed the American's innate anti-statist sentiments but the visitor still delightfully shocks at their intensity, instincts, and ingrainedness. There is, it should be said, an almost obsessive fear of a powerful executive that grips most tightly the individual here. I find a remarkable definiteness in the dogma of the sovereignty of the individual. These matters were first noted by the French aristocrat de Tocqueville when he reported the commitment to the historically exceptional investment of sovereignty in the people.

But the American is not merely unlikely to look on the state as either the provider of benefits or the guarantor of equal outcomes; he is a man far more oriented in his daily dealings to the market and a nature of enterprise probable. He cannot conceal his contempt and aversion for regulation or taxation; his nature revealing its thick libertarian stripes, even if the outsider cannot help but feel such stripes are quixotic. It becomes most rapidly apparent that the American is a man most loyal to the notions of equality and egalitarianism but only in its genuine form; he believes in equality of birth, not equality of result. The individualism of this land runs deep, I must concede; it is reflected even in the least accurate representative of the American: his movie industry. Seldom exists the major motion picture without the plot involving the vigilante main character; a male or female disregarding of police or government agencies, authorities often painted as corrupt, unhelpful or incompetent; story lines that may even require the character in pursuit of vigilante justice to fight such authority along the way. It is clear to the outsider that the fictional stops with its events; there is scant doubt that seeds of sympathy for such action exist in all but very few Americans. The more frank of American men happily explain to the outsider that great acts of individualism are heroic, patriotic and integral to the national identity.

The Value of Liberty

It is hard for me to conceive of a man more jealous of his liberty; freedom is the first noun or adjective of choice offered when he describes his land. I cannot stress the ubiquity of the term in the life, culture and public discourse among these men: its emphasis is confronting. Even the visitor of the Western nation that might consider themselves free (although the American is quick to remind that they are anything but) is largely unaccustomed to hearing the term, if he is honest; such is the rarity of its use in those nations, even in the language of their political representatives. The American considers himself, rightfully, I hasten to add, not only the embodiment of human freedom but also the model for individual liberty. It seems that over here man is rendered almost incapable of taking freedom and his Republic for granted through the substantial militaristic presence in his national culture. The American conceives, again rightfully, that freedom is not free, an assertion he makes often wiping away a tear; the visitor is immediately moved by how touched he is by the enormous price his nation has paid to spread or defend his values and ideals.

The fidelity of the American to individual liberty, the visitor finds, is exceptional in its sincerity. I can report that the man of this land is deeply aware liberty may carry unequal outcome yet he remains committed to its pursuit; a genuine faith as opposed to the counterfeit devotion common in the other lands of the Western world, where commitment to liberty is conditional on the outcome of equality. The American suffers no such imposter; his belief in liberty even if variant unquestionable. The visitor is reminded of the Civil War of the nineteenth century in the context of liberty, when here as elsewhere, the American showed the exception that proves the rule where two competing ideas of liberty collided and ultimately fused.

The new immigrant of this nation is shockingly stirring and almost erudite when he recounts his choice to make home in this land. He speaks assuredly of the self-belief, surety, and system of values present here as if he had not lived one day without them. He breathlessly intones the opportunity of the nation, a product explained by him to be only possible with and by the principles of the American society, as the most compelling of his motivations. It is not for denial that this nation is the mostly highly desired for living than all; it is almost tangible to the outsider that from sunlight to sunset, the number in this land increase. It is a boast of the American that his nation accepts more legal immigrants as permanent residents every year than all of the other nations of the world combined. Yet it strikes the visitor with sudden force that despite these great swathes of men and women of most diverse lands and personality, their assimilation here is faster and calmer than any other community. It is at this point that I am left with no other determination than this: it is the strength of this prized set of values that stands this nation on the shoulders of others.

It is clear that in light of the American experience and that of his Western cousins, the diluted, unconfident and directionless culture, with its dearth of reference to values, is most poisonous to any integration objective for new immigrants. Indeed, as any Western visitor can attest of his homeland: it is a democracy riddled with equivocation, where the immigrant is, at best, able to make vague reference to a "better life" or at worst, and the latter is far more common, insistent on preserving their place of origin to the point where it exceeds parity with their current culture.

But perhaps most fascinating in the American is his unwritten contract or community covenant between him and those that choose his land. I have quickly discovered that the American has not the luxury of automatic unity or the deep roots of birth or blood and his choice of compensation is most unique. His contract appears both disinterested and uninterested in the background or beliefs of the prospective American; it is, in fact, conspicuously elegant and logical in its simplicity and brevity. The visitor learns that it comprises of a sole requirement resting squarely on the shoulders of the party desiring life in a new land. It requires only that the incoming immigrant exhibit loyalty to the ideals of its new country, and ensures that he or she will be affectionately welcomed. It appears on the surface a most flimsy agreement, the kind a man of the law would never advise being signatory to, yet the yields of the great experiment must be conceded: a bond of greater strength in the history of world civilization cannot be found. The mere reliance on the unity of a transcendental set of values formulating citizenship is evidence of the American's propensity to great risk for enormous reward.

The values that I speak of in this country are a lifestyle that fortify the patriot and unity; circumstances exceptional to him and this land. It is not to say that the American does not welcome the new perspective or the fresh influence; after all, his is a self-made society, and much like the self-made man, he readjusts and renews with great dexterity. But amidst this elasticity, the American, and his contract, do certainly put this nation first, in typically absolutist terms. This palpable precept, the outsider feels, is a powerful exterminator of the noxious weed of home-grown terrorism.

It is a substance most difficult to communicate but the visitor is struck by a certain youthfulness that exists, an almost rawness in the man and his land here; one that might perhaps be found in the adolescent state of man. It seems that these raw elements in the finished product of the individual and culture are the reason that his values transform to self-evident truths. I must say, it feels often when speaking to the man here, that his personality is reminiscent of the biggest and strongest seventeen-year-old star football player of the local school, belonging to a family of committed Christians. The American holds his values as tightly and patently true as may be expected of such a student; both men are far more inclined to fight passionately on their behalf than the graying and mature adult.

It can be surmised that the uniqueness of this land in having been intentionally brought into being should ensure that these somewhat coarse but certainly adolescent trademarks are retained for the life of this nation; it would appear at first glance that any departure from this would surely end the domination of this man and his country. It would be remiss, however, to not note that his values have to this juncture exhibited remarkable and unprecedented staying power. He has thus far repelled the external forces of elite culture, refusing to succumb to their utopian temptations, and the idea that no set of values is worth defending, although dangers are visible on the horizon. Should the American follow the fate of the Romans,

Byzantines, Abbasids, Ottomans, and Khans, or the once magnificent nations of Old Europe, by disintegrating into the dusk of moral and cultural decadence, there is little doubt that his fall from grace will be the most spectacular and steep of all.

I must say that the man of this land in general possesses a healthy paranoia; a defense system that he shows regularly to have capacity to identify even the seemingly benign and innocuous piloted in stealth. The cultural beast of relativism struggles to prey here in the American jungle; the man here sensing intuitively the myopia of relativism, considering it the moral equivalent of cannabis. This perspective protects the American largely from fateful compromise with the ideologies of other men that conflict with those of his founders. The visitor can only presume based on his observation that the man of this nation is unassailable if his abiding commitment to his values subsists; the fate of failure in his own hands.

There is many the man of the foreign land, and perhaps some in this one, that declare that I and the man of this land today operate in a post-American world. I can find no reason to believe this to be in the least true; the visitor to this land still senses the grandness of this land with his every step. It is impossible to be on this soil among exceptional men without the feeling of exhilaration and hope; the American excites the soul and senses of man like no other. It is, though, clear in the faces of these people that they are in hard times, and the visitor can well see, based on his knowledge of the past, that the American is falling behind his own potential. The visitor feels that the pressure point of his pain is in the pursuit of action or movement, by some of his number, inconsistent with his founding or values. This is not to discount the unusually high expectations of the man of this land held by the people of the world are surpassed only by his own; it is why the usually upbeat American today finds himself with somewhat slumped shoulders. But the man who propagates the end of this man's cultural dominance does so at great peril or with desperate hope, or both. I am forced to conclude, even in the light of American worry and when this man and his land are nearing their lowest ebb, that the culture of this land called America is just at the infancy of her power, a most heartening creed for humanity. This century may impose far greater challenge and graver threat to it than the last but this, too, will surely be an American century.

Chapter 2
OLD GLORY

The propensity of the man of this society for the conservation of the natural never ceases to stun; it is a partiality that transcends the malleability he exhibits in other areas. It is most true that loving one's nation is perhaps only second in rank to service to country; a virtue chiseled in the bedrock of morality. As the natural state of man is love of his country; a citizenry ready to pay the ultimate sacrifice for their country has been the long-held expectation. To fathom a nation more defined by its borders, language and culture than the American is most challenging; a deliberate construct most abhorrent to the internationalist tendencies of the day. Few men of the world could refute the steady and sustained attack on the virtue of patriotism since the conclusion of the last world war. It is today mostly considered by the men of the West as poor form; an out-dated, anti-intellectual, prejudicial, bellicose, and even immoral, state.

The American is the most patriotic of men; within this land, the virtue is deep and horizontal. In this nation resides a most discernible common language of citizenship just as notable absent in the other lands, spoken in a multifarious constituency with variant accent and irregular syntax, but always retaining its commonality. It is at once impressive, inescapable and infectious to the visitor, perhaps the most exceptional of attributes of this culture and people. The man in this country has doubtlessly been shaped by the events of the twentieth century; the older American explains that his patriotism and nationalism deepened greatly during the two World Wars. But most interestingly is this man's anxious preoccupation with communism; the outsider finds the sentiment a matter of virtual national identity. There is not a man here, irrespective of his political leaning, unwilling to unleash savagely, without a moment's hesitation or the slightest provocation, on the evils of the communistic agenda. I have not the thinnest of doubt that these entrenched anti-communist predilections are the consequences of the Cold War, and I must again marvel at the American's aptitude, whether by deliberate or accidental design, in shaping his society to great advantage.

The man here understands patriotism, like language, is social and cultural glue. The American rightfully considers no aspect more fundamental to the success of a nation than that of the patriotic; he has witnessed in his years the pervasive effect it has on every facet of human nature. From his birth until his death, the outsider must conclude that it is the patriotism of the man here responsible for his confidence and incentive to excel with exception. The visitor can only speculate on the effects of such widespread nationalism within education.

If the American is to be properly understood, and his greatness appreciated, his patriotism cannot be avoided; it must feature highly in any series of cultural analyses. I cannot stress with sufficient emphasis the life it affords the man here; his unity, strength, inclusion and dominance of the world in every field are born of and rest with it. But these circumstances that the American has manufactured may be unique, but they are hardly fixed. The refurbishment of the glue in a polity must always top the national priority, and so it is here; the American devoting many of his hours to creative thought and sustained action in achieving this noble objective. The patriotism of this land differs from tradition by way of its potency; its roots firmly planted in the transcendent values of individual freedom, Christianity, justice, and democracy.

The American considers each achievement of his country a personal victory. But more than this: he appears entirely unselfish in remembering his nation at all times. The man here seems prone to nostalgia, almost born with the keenest of eyes to his history and democratic beginning. I must say of the American: he possesses in him a philosophical depth, recognizing that history is to the nation as memory is to the individual. Any earnest conversation with him reveals he understands well that man cannot tell where he is today or where he will find himself tomorrow, unless he knows from where he has come.

The man here, conditioned only in vigorous patriotism from birth, is unaware that many of his displays and modes of nationalistic expression are exclusive to him. What the American refers to as "The Pledge of Allegiance" is perhaps the greatest example of his exceptionalism in this regard. A string of thirty-one words, recited by citizens standing and facing the American flag, with their right hands over their hearts, it succinctly encapsulates the fervor and flavor of the American patriotic condition. The visitor will rarely find a man, woman, or child anywhere in this land unable to recite the words of the Pledge; the American starts any events or meetings of any standing with it, and the schoolchild recites it daily. It is a most stimulating and unforgettable experience to stand amid Americans of all stripes at the beginning of public events and meetings, witnessing firsthand the swift, automatic shuffle of feet and pivoting of collective bodies in the direction of the hanging American flag. For a form of words recited so often, it could be thought that the words would be recited automatically, free of emotion. Yet I delighted with immeasurable surprise at the voices invariably ringing with passion and the earnest faces, fixed eyes, stern concentration commensurate with the gravity of the words. From a cacophony of voices came a united chorus; a most rousing experience for the unsuspecting visitor.

The most common and recognizable sight across this gigantic land is the American flag. Such is the love of the national flag here, it is affectionately referred to as "Old Glory," a term first coined by patriot William Driver, a nineteenth-century sea captain. It must be said that the visibility of a country's flag within its own borders is a measure of greatness and strength. The simple action of a man flying his flag outside his home in other lands, even those of the English language, is considered at best, aberrant, a glaring contrast to the sprightly patriotic activity of the man here. His veneration for his flag staggers the visitor; the American deploring any slovenly treatment of it. The protocols that exist in this nation regarding the display and care of the flag are most extraordinary. Incomparable in detail, they exist for its folding, displaying, hanging, and carrying; every occasion, location, and context covered, ranging from the procession to the funeral, the car to the home, mourning to celebration, the podium to the window, and the location of the flag when present with others. It should be, in this light, of little surprise that from the foothills of the Appalachians in North Carolina to steamy Louisiana and the deserts of Texas to the Rockies of New Mexico, and all over, the flag of this nation is truly ubiquitous. As the visitor crisscrosses

Exceptional America

the small towns and big cities, irrespective of population or demography, he finds flags adorning streets, shopping centers, buildings, homes, graves, letterboxes, taxis, buses, cars, and petrol stations. I must underline: these are not simply temporary decorations for the national day; they are permanent fixtures of patriotic pride. Faced with such overwhelming patriotic abundance, I cannot shake the strange sense of reassurance, comfort and inclusion, this land to which I am foreign, fills me. With this overpowering effect on a mere short-staying visitor, the consequences for the American psyche can only be speculated.

This is to forget to mention the omnipresence of the colors of red, white and blue, those on his flag, in everyday life. Favored by business, sports and entrepreneurs, the national colors, with often accompanying stars and stripes, find themselves on logos, mascots, shop facades, and products. This sea of red, white, and blue, the visitor finds, is further augmented with the boatloads of reference to founding principles and countless symbols and emblems.

There is said to be almost 3.8 million square miles of soil of this land and I am of no doubt that there is not a stretch within it without a location bearing a name of historical or cultural connection. It is most probable that streets, restaurants, buildings, businesses, towns, schools, hotels, and cities of this man are named such; liberty, independence, constitution and freedom the most common. To provide a state-specific name in the title of an organization located in an entirely different part of this land is most usual, as is to honor the famous man in his home state through names.

Upon later reflection, in the privacy of his own space, it is beyond the bounds of possibility for the visitor to do little but shake his head in admiration at the exceptional elements of the patriotism in this country. The man here once more seems ahead with his intuition, understanding that repetition is the motherhood of retention; the crucial element ensuring the extensive travel of patriotism within a culture and the culminating permeation through to the public and private life of individuals. In color, pledge, names and flag, the American clearly conceives repetition and metastasis as continuous cycles, feeding from each other, producing unceasing reminders of his history. I must say his resulting environment is most stunning; the man here resides in a virtual bubble, an overwhelmingly reassuring environment, one which engenders in him the irrepressible judgment he exists in the heart and center of the world, requiring nothing else. The side effect of such pervasive patriotism is insularity, but it is easy to excuse the man here, living in the most diverse, both geographic and ethnic, and exceptional land, for his provincial viewpoint.

As it has been previously mentioned, the man here struggles, understandably, to appreciate the exceptionalism of his patriotism given his conviction that it is the inherent state of man, and is unlikely to attribute his elevation over other men to it. It must also be said that the same struggle appears in the average man of the nation of limited pride, unity or patriotism; he is unbothered by it as he knows no better, impervious to the personal and collective straitjacket that such circumstances produce. It is only the unique outsider, or visitor, wrought with ambition or established success, with a penchant for risk that can pinpoint the limitations of such society. The words of international English sports star, David Beckham, should most certainly make their way to the man of this land for him to fully appreciate and preserve his patriotic proclivity:

Exceptional America

> I've been lucky to have been a pretty regular visitor to America since I was a boy. Time enough to get to know a country that I've grown to love . . . . If I could take one aspect of American life back to England with me, it would be this country's sense of patriotism; the feeling of a whole nation united under one flag. Maybe the pride Americans take in their country is one of the reasons why sports stars here seem to enjoy a level of respect that's not always the case in Europe. Heroes of mine like Michael Jordan, Tiger Woods, Andre Agassi and Michael Johnson have been pushed on to greater achievement, I'd say, because they know they've got the unqualified support of the whole country behind them when they go into action. These sporting greats have taken advantage of being born and raised in the land of opportunity. The American Dream is founded on the same principles as my own: if you work hard enough, there never needs to be a limit on how far life can take you.

Over here, the man of America conflates the American dream with his patriotism; the two are inseparable in these parts. I must say that the personality of the men of this continent is unlike any other. I find him bereft of reservation; he is a man of the most penetrating passion, optimism and emotion. He projects each of these in his every communication, particularly when he communicates his patriotism. The moist eye and the hand covering the heart may be seized upon by intelligentsia for ridicule but the visitor here realizes these are mere modes of this man's natural expression. The American refreshes in his enthusiasm; his sporting events a moving spectacle where athletes and crowds sing their national anthem with all the intensity and concentration they can muster. I must say it is a most different experience to the equivalent of other lands. It may appear to the serious man a trivial example but it is nevertheless most enlightening. A visit to this land reveals that it is most devoid of the common and prevalent self-destructive quality within the national character of other nations. But it must also be noted that man here is yet to be feminized, and thus speaks candidly with volume; he is often aggressive and always fearless, valuing the masculine traits of confidence and force of his crusading ethos, in his patriotic proclamation.

It is greatly difficult to not admire the American; a man unafraid to speak of his greatness. It is equally demanding to fault or condemn this culture, where overt displays of pride are mainstream, and encouraged. Testament to the strength and resilience of the American is his marginalization of the moral and cultural relativist elite threatened most by patriotic passion. The man here has little truck for those that deliberately paint his prized patriotism as an attitude of the simplistic, uneducated, slack-jawed redneck said to be feverishly practicing the arts of jingoism and xenophobia in the dark hours of the morning.

As one may contemplate in the early hours of the day, it dawns on him that the enormous success and ambition of this national project is made all the more inspiring by the population of this land, large and diverse, yet harmonious. Where other continents have sought the division of nations into micro-states to resolve matters of conflict, this land of most assorted men shows not the slightest need for such action.

The Melting Pot

The American never forgets his country, no matter where in the world he may find himself. I had heard prior to coming here stories of this man's commitment to his nation. It was shared with me by a friend who, while studying in China, roomed with a Californian student, in a university dorm. This young man approached my friend, expressing a desire to hang up his American flag on the outside of their door. The approach was polite but firm and confident, and my friend felt unable to express any opposition to a suggestion put so reasonably. My friend was amazed at the intense pride in his country that had inspired his roommate to carry his flag half way around the world and his eagerness to proclaim it in a foreign country. Visiting this nation and becoming accustomed to its mores, such tales surprise little but it must be said that the excitement of the patriotism in this land wanes not even for the seasoned visitor.

Imbedded in the grand seal of the United States of America is *E pluribus unum*, the Latin phrase for "Out of many, one." There is, to the visitor, no phrase that perhaps better accounts or reflects the exceptional mentality and society of this man than this. This man is most unlike any other I have come across: it is as if he has been schooled in the opposite way to the man of the other nations. Where other men have been conditioned to emphasize the differences of immigrant cultures and conditioned to ignore the formidable worth unity, no evidence of this ailment exists in any part of the American. He may be of malleable materials as a self-made man but he is immovable in the face of cultural pluralism. His fixed eye on national unity and its virtues appears to be deeply embedded; inherited eyesight of his founding fathers. I read with interest in the libraries of this nation the American's Federalist Papers, and I note in the second of these Papers, written by the first American Supreme Court Chief Justice, John Jay, and published on October 31, 1787, his words:

> Providence has been pleased to give this one connected country to one united people—a people descended from the same ancestors, speaking the same language, professing the same religion, attached to the same principles of government, very similar in their manners and customs . . . This country and this people seem to have been made for each other, and it appears as if it was the design of Providence, that an inheritance so proper and convenient for a band of brethren, united to each other by the strongest ties, should never be split into a number of unsocial, jealous, and alien sovereignties.

I astound at his prescience; his foresight to identify the erosion of the distinctive culture of a host nation and the weakening, indeed potential collapse, of the nation state entity is beyond extraordinary. But it is in the study of this man's ancestors that the visit truly begins to comprehend the enormity of the American mind.

Here the immigrant must assimilate to mainstream society by surrendering their differences; a self-proclaimed hyphenated American is treated with suspicion and derision, and the visitor feels little sympathy. It is clear in this land that a hyphenated identity is most antithetical; un-American, if the term were to exist. The allegiance to a foreign nation other than that of their home may be common in the citizens of other nations but the American recoils at the prospect. It has been labeled a "melting pot" by many a commentator, and so it feels even vicariously. Such nomenclature is most fitting, and indeed synonymous with this land, but most significantly, you cannot help but feel when here, it is the source of the ultimate manifestation of American power and patriotism. This pot of the American stove is a utensil most redolent with the undertones of his exceptionalism. In the cultural cafeteria of this land, with its exhaustive menu of options designed for every taste, the American is a most loyal subject. If ever the marketers of the world desired a successful model on which to base their work, I must say they should look not past this land for this man exhibits the outcomes of a confident and strong national identity, with unequivocal and highly marketed values. If there is only one thing to learn from this man, it is that it is only in the context of the unconfident national culture that the citizen search for alternative identities to that which is in their passport.

Based on the experience in this country, one must determine that it is only where immigrants are expected to submit to the dominant culture of their new home that cohesion, success and the exceptional can flourish. As I travel through the vastness of this land, I see new immigrants and Mayflower descendants alike, glued together by the English language, a belief in the American dream, and the values of freedom, justice, and equality of birth but not outcome.

Even the immigrant to this land thinks differently; he considers that he is owed nothing and seeks not an auxiliary service, maintaining his survival and success are matters if choice and personal work. The visitor in these dialogues is startled at the compatibility of such thought with the American dream and again struck by the immense disparity of the immigrant of other industrialized nations who is bathed in demand and expectation. I am struck by the reality and potential of my finding that the immigrant population and their descendants, found on every stretch of soil here, have enriched and flourished it. The cultural covenant of this land today seems almost incapable of educing ingratitude, indifference and antagonism amongst any of its people, the very elements causing of a nation to flounder.

The ethnic heritage of a man in this land remains only in his last name; its absence conspicuous in his personality, interest, and moral compass. He shows, at best, scant curiosity in the heritage of his ancestry, and never raises it in conversation. Indeed, he finds the raising of it in conversation most odd, perplexed that it would be a subject on which to dwell for some. Unlike the men of other nations, the American does not consider it lasting, consequential or inescapable, but merely a matter of trivia. It occasions no surprise that he bears such perspective; after all, it is the view of this man that he is not defined, whether by limit or certain traits, of the circumstances of his birth. He, an individual, is what he chooses to be.

I can deem the position of these Americans on these matters of culture nothing other than logical; it is a matter of reason that a host nation has the superior hand. It is, after all, the choice of men not born here to come and I am left asking who could blame them. Those men seek the values, opportunities and lifestyle of the American. While the American tends to be a remarkably insular man, he displays an almost unmatched recognition of this, assuring me that he is undisposed to bending his social fabric for any minority. It is not unusual to stumble across the American who puts it in confrontational terms: he is unwilling to lose the war

Exceptional America

to the very people who are benefiting from the hundreds years of freedom his nation and its English-speaking cousins secured. These assurances are not offered lightly as matters of preference; the visitor identifies them as vehement opinion, fearlessly and publically expressed.

The man in this nation continually intimidates with his unprecedented clarity of thought; he appears more disposed to logic than any other. No greater illustration of this can be found than his verdict on cultural diversity; he understands almost uniquely that it is a means to an end but not an end in and of itself. His analysis conceives the folly in believing in everything; he understands that believing in everything amounts to believing in nothing, a rational deduction seemingly elusive in the world beyond these borders. It is in this way that the American differentiates himself; he believes in certain things to the exclusion of others.

It is his morality that derives his patriotic soul, and even on this innate level, I am reminded of this man's incompatibility with the elite men of universities, and his tendency to offend the tastes of their narrow palate; men who posit that moral belief be impartial and universal. The visitor here discovers a most clear symbiosis between God and country; a combination more defiant of the elite unimaginable.

The state of unity is only delivered when shared values are emphatically embraced; patriotism is the key principal of political legitimacy. The outside visitor finds that the cultural spotlight of this land on unity is echoed by the public communication of the democratically elected leaders of this country, reflecting not simply audience will, but the path deemed most conducive to securing votes. Such circumstances do little else but bewilder the outsider for he is accustomed to vastly different approaches. The equivalent representatives in his land, and indeed those of all nations across the two oceans that safeguard this land, seldom refer to unity, preferring to adhere to the divide and conquer strategy, with great effect, it must be said.

There is outspoken concern held by the man of this nation that his patriotism is no longer as ardent as it once was and that his malleability has extended somewhat to surfaces previously immobile. It is most challenging for the visitor to judge current levels of patriotism here to the past but the man here should take comfort that he is merely falling behind his potential, not any other nation.

There are, however, more discernible dangers within the range of the outside eye, and it should be noted, visible to the American. In many parts of this land walked by the visitor, it is as frequent to hear the Spanish language as it is the English, but this fact is not nearly as concerning to the American as the government recognition offered to it. The visitor is puzzled that the famed logic of the American fails him here; it cannot be denied that to become active in public discourse and engage in the life of this land, the ability to read and speak in English is not open for negotiation.

Any man should sleep restlessly when the schools of his children and the representatives of his community advance relativism, and many of the men here do. It is disappointing that those who do not fail to call upon their seemingly innate philosophical depth and the prescience of their founders to recognize the rational: a society does not survive if it has no reason to. The man of this nation must, both in the home and in the school, pass on to his young the meaning of his country. As I navigate through this country, I feel this task the great calling of this man's time, no less than his history at stake.

Exceptional America

There are unconscionable numbers of men that cross the borders of this nation illegally daily; the American appearing uncharacteristically helpless in quelling such lawlessness. This is compounded by the advocacy of the deeply misguided thankfully few, for the moral code and religious law of the Islamic to have recognition in this land. The latter matter is at this time, only significant insofar as it suggests to the outsider the man of this nation will not be immune and must prepare himself for these challenges. The American must remember that men of any country are never further away than the distance of relativism to graceless and unsavory acts of public disorder ignited by racial or community division.

I am confident in the men of this country but most assured by their history, and its proven bold boomerang quality. I have little doubt that the American will realize in time that to bow to the dictates of the elite and follow the paths of men in nations that have is to radically alter his land and transform his culture as one which will make him feel most unwelcome.

He must exercise fidelity to his homogeneous creation, one that has delivered exceptional accomplishment and heed the prescient warnings of his magnificent founders. One cannot help but find the nature of this man's exceptionalism deeply bemusing; only his brilliant mind could marry, in exactly equal proportion of influence within the same house, cultural homogeneity and individual diversity.

Chapter 3

FAITH

I find of this country that, as the world of the West practices secular humanism with fervor deserving of a religion, the man here is fluent in his Christian faith. It is true that the entire American experience is irrevocably connected through Christianity; religious observance most common throughout the land.

The institutional and legal exceptionalism of this nation is perhaps best exemplified in the form of the Constitution; a document guaranteeing, in this case, the religious freedom of each man that inhabits the terrain of its jurisdiction. But while this may be falsely seized by the relativist, secularist or non-Christian man to assert that this is not a Christian nation, any good-natured visitor here can only offer laughter to such absurdity. I cannot insist in stronger terms to this; I am unable to conceive a land and its men with greater priority or passion for Christ; primacy that appears to the outsider as permanent and panoptic. While I am careful to not offend the American man of this view and therefore do not labor the point, I must say, albeit reluctantly, my interpretation of the First Amendment of the Constitution is radically different to his. Where he sees its purpose as the protection of man and his law from religious values; I see

Exceptional America

it as the protection of those very values from the oppressive tyranny of government.

The strong Christian faith of the man here is least confounding when it is considered that his very nation was founded on the Christian view of man and government that prevailed at the time. It is true that there were two or three Founding fathers in the minority preferring of an atheistic path reminiscent of the French revolutionaries; so it is not to say that this country is Christian because all of its founders were and people are: it is because of the then contemporary majority Christian view of man and government. The intent to forge a nation under God is most clear to the reader of the Declaration of Independence, the Constitution and Bill of Rights, the American's famous texts.

These historic matters do not appear lost on the man here, with a deep and abiding Christian faith infinite in the culture of this land, and integral to the formation of an assertive civil religion. I am left with no option but to believe the American must have been entirely disconnected to the religious skepticism of the Enlightenment for I see not a fingerbreadth of evidence otherwise. The capital of this nation, a city named after the greatest American of them all, is covered with references to God and faith by past leaders of this land. As the visitor sights these tributes, walking from one to the other, he feels the Christian roots underneath the soil upon which he treads; a sentiment only reinforced by the revelations of these sites of the faith of past leaders and their seeking of providential assistance and advice in making decisions, fusing the anxiety with optimism.

Nick Adams

A Duty to Uphold

Commensurate with this adaptability, the history of the American suggests his civic religion intensifies when he sees the effects of the atheistic or evil; it was in the decade following the Second World War that his patriotism was not the only virtue to be bolstered; it was accompanied by the dramatic increase in his civic religion. I am reminded by the older American here of the action of President Eisenhower who, in a bid to differentiate formally this land from the godless union of the Soviet, added the words "Under God" to the Pledge of Allegiance in 1954. Upon doing so, he said,

> In this way, we are reaffirming the transcendence of religious faith in America's heritage and future; in this way we shall constantly strengthen those spiritual weapons which forever will be our country's most powerful resource in peace and war.

I, nor any man, can deny that the attributes of Christian worship arm the American with emotion and self-belief, requisite qualities for any world leader. The visitor finds in this land that Christianity is consumed; it soothes its cultural soul and heals the national heart. The man here is most cognizant of the curative role his religion can play even in his internal national matters; the aftermath of his Civil War and the prejudice associated with the Civil Rights movement.

The man here, in what no visitor would consider or describe a godforsaken place, has demonstrated throughout his history the truth of the words of Eisenhower and the success of the Christian faith, when featured in the life of the individual and his institution; he need only offer the visitor the superb example of his nation, one with the greatest degree of liberty, prosperity, creativity, optimism, success, and peace, as his evidence. The American cleverly juxtaposes to the outsider his experience and God-fearing character to the yields of the avowed atheism of the previous century. It is certainly true that where avowed atheism delivered the two most murderous regimes of the previous century, Nazi Germany and the Soviet Union, Christianity has permitted his nation to be the dynamic torch of liberty, and the ultimate citadel upon which dreams of tyranny and oppression are shattered.

Much in the same vein of his patriotism, and true to the word of the Gospel, God is omnipresent in this land, to the visitor and American alike. He is there every time the American, or for that matter, the visitor, reaches into his pocket; his national motto "In God We Trust" inscribed on his coins and printed on his notes. The political leaders of this land are incapable of delivering a significant oration without the concluding refrain of which involves "God bless America." The outsider, unaccustomed to references to deity in community occasions or public life, delights in the ubiquity of God at these events, uplifted in receipt of inspiration. The religious heritage and nature of this country is exceptional yet provocative. It feels at times that the man of this nation is permanently set on a collision course with a great many, not least of which, is the secular left ideology of which many of his allied nations have embraced.

The religious character and heritage of America make it utterly contrarian to the secular left ideology currently recently embraced by the Western world. The problem with the atheist is not that he will believe in nothing but that he will believe in anything. The American can be religiously diverse; Christianity is not the only religion of his nation, a deliberate consequence of his founding. But with the same success as his cultural melting pot of *E pluribus unum*, the different religions of the American co-exist across this nation with unique and seemly peace; largely a result of the combined society the American has fostered, in which interreligious association occurs in perpetuity. Unlike those polities of the outsider nations, separated within by culture and religion, the American is exceptional.

It should be noted that the intensity of the religion of this land is variant, largely dependent on location; the two brackets of its coastline participate comparatively less. But even in these communities of the Far East and West, I feel they are more molded by the overpowering national sentiment than which they may be prepared to concede. It is, however, with certainty, a myth that the man of fervent religiosity hails only from the deep south of this nation; the committed Christian scattered like seeds in and across every direction.

There is, it is undeniable, an alliterative God-gap between those societies of which I am accustomed and this. The Christianity that sweeps this nation almost uniformly is most distinguishing. The man here most likely to attend church at least once a week, a powerful contrast to his cousins in the west. The visiting outsider notes with interest that the nation of which most of the American's ancestors fled is today in spiritual vacuum, circumstances first identified by prescient novelist, C.S. Lewis in his work *The Screwtape Letters*. But it is not only the English-speaking man that has turned his back on religion; the other nations of Europe barren in faith, the men of the continent shunning Christianity in record number. It should be noted that this is a recent departure, for it was the western European man of the sixteenth century that set the course for Christianity to once more propel to dominance yet today it feels as if the man of this land is on his own.

I must point out that the Christian man here is not of the mere census variety; that is to say, he does not merely identify, he believes and belongs. He is more aptly described as a cultural Christian, with formidable evidence of commitment to the faith in his national psyche, tangibly different to the census version of the faith that exists in the homes of many of his Western relatives. There is certainly of this land a distinctly religious character, and it is to the mind of the observer, the primary reason that in this land creativity triumphs over destruction and hope presides over despair. The virtues and values of the men here are seeded in Christianity.

It surprises the visitor little that the man here clasps to his Christian faith most tightly; he is particularly subject to the natural disasters whose effects make little or no sense in their specific consequences, allowing him to draw the conclusion that there is a grand plan for him by his Creator. He here is subject to almost all forms of natural disasters, almost constantly. In fact, there is no other nation in the world, with the exception of the American cousin, Australia, albeit it with far less men, subject to the number, scale and diversity of the cataclysmic event. The American seems to understand better than any other man the wrath of God, through his own experiences if he lived in what this man calls Tornado Alley or elsewhere.

Nick Adams

A Public Faith

I doubt not for one moment that this man and his values are fortified by the profundity of his Christianity; the American hiding not even remotely that he is lifted and reassured by God, or that he as his past leaders did, seeks providential help for his life, and even this nation. If it were to be asked of the visitor to name the virtues of the American man directly attributable to his religion, it would be these: optimism, morality, courage, confidence, clarity, and strength.

It is not uncommon to see the American saying grace in a public eatery; such an act I have found is more often than not a staple in a private setting. The man here engages in prayer, both individually and collectively; he is a most devoted believer in intercessory prayer. It strikes me that I cannot think of another act drawing of such simultaneous action. I have determined that the man of this nation, unlike any other I have met, will only choose collectivist action over his own individualism, when a moral imperative radiating from his faith, impels him to. The moralistic focus of the culture here, borne of the Puritan, forms with individualism to produce an exceptional elixir to inherent conflict. It is only this that can explain why this land of the individual is also the country of the excelling collective; matters the observer finds most difficult at first to reconcile. The home of the finest military and most indivisible unity, evidence of grand collective effort, is hardly a collectivist nation; to the contrary, it is a land of unequaled emphatic individualism. This exception land allows for only one conclusion: a team of individuals super-glued by the moral imperative of their personal faith will always trump the mediocrity of a team of banal collectivists. The moral imperative of which I speak and that which the Christian faith provides the American man is the same that prompted de Tocqueville's most pithy and memorable assertion:

> America is great because she is good, and if America ever ceases to be good, America will cease to be great.

But in all his extensive writings on religion in this land, I feel it was when de Tocqueville offered the following that he was at his finest:

> I sought for the greatness and genius of America in her commodious harbours and her ample rivers, and it was not there. In the fertile fields and boundless prairies, and it was not there. In her rich mines and her vast world commerce, and it was not there. Not until I went into the churches of America and heard her pulpits, aflame with righteousness, did I understand the secret of her genius and power.

For all the travel that has carried me to every corner, quarter and pocket of this land, from west to east and north to south and everything in between, I can but only agree with de Tocqueville for his thesis of this man's exceptionalism. Even today with the American having propelled himself forward with such magnitude and force in all conceivable fields, it is only when one visits the churches and sits in the pews with this man that the greatness of him and his land is to be apprehended or digested. The experience will strike the soul of any man, leaving even the most atheistic of his breed inspired and refreshed; it is surely is one of the great moments of humanity, the type impossible to ever relinquish from memory.

The churches here are incomparable to any I have previously entered; they overflow with charisma and drip with life. The man in these churches appears to have little regard for silence, formality or restraint, unless the circumstances require him so. The sight of worship here is one to behold; the visitor is, at first, astonished by what he witnesses. His eyes and ears are greeted with men and women in boisterous song of uplifting sound with upwardly stretched palms and tapping feet, often swaying. Here even the disabled and elderly American rocks slowly rocks forward and back, as if trapped in trance. I cannot help but admire these men and women who dance, sing and move as if celebrating the simple treasure of life. Even as the leader of the church speaks here, the men of his congregation nod their vigorous approval, often declaring aloud with spontaneity his agreement.

In the man here there is an uncommon level of emotion, indisputably a product of his religiosity. The Christian of this country has a forthrightness in faith, and a willingness to share his disposition I have seldom encountered. These are conditions most unusual for even the non-census, genuine Christian of other lands; a man reserved and quiet in his faith. Religion is quite openly discussed by the men of this nation; they appear the least encumbered of men by the view of the subject as a delicate. It is for this reason that I find the American to communicate his faith fearlessly and frankly; a trait, it strikes me, most consistent with the teachings of the New Testament: the spreading of good news.

As I muse these matters, I reach the conclusion that the longevity, and indeed burgeoning, of the Christian faith is owed, in no small part, to the characteristics of religion in this nation. But I do not believe the physiognomy of the faith existing here can be replicated elsewhere; it relies heavily on the persona of the American, a product of the unique culture, intrinsically variant to that of other men. In the culture more valuing of a collectivist sentiment, the outward public expression of faith, a distinguishing mark of differentiation, is unwelcome and discomforting. I cannot see how such a church could survive the personality of such men, for whom fear overrides honesty to actualize mainstream silence, formed within the climes of free speech with consequences.

I do not suggest even momentarily that the church experience is identical throughout this land; it is largely dependent on denomination, size, and location. But the church of charisma here is a native species of the American; I cannot imagine such a place anywhere in the world other than here. This type of church, of which I speak, is often gigantic in size, filled with numbers on a Sunday morning unfathomable to the outsider; some thousands, others in the tens of thousands. These numbers can simply not be apportioned to the extensive population of the man here; it is much more than that. If ever informed of these unconscionable quantities of men in attendance before visiting here, I would have been most dubious, and considered the impersonality of such church to be of detraction. But I would not have been more wrong; the American always one step ahead, with religious leaders ensuring there are smaller groups within, promoting, in fact, the most personal and tight of social setting, imperative for the satisfaction of the American's faith. The religious leader thinks like a businessman in this land; he accounts in large part for the innovation so integral to religion here. There seems to always be an incessant flow of such innovation where the man he adapts his practice and receipt of religion to reflect the modern modes of communication.

With the thinking of the religious leader reminiscent of the man of commerce, it surprises in the least that in this land capitalism combines Christianity. There is no shortage here of choice for a place to worship; the visitor is astounded to find, even the remotest and tiniest of the communities of this man, multiple places of worship. I find an open and healthy competition exists between them, each using innovation to flourish their church, enhance their service and increase their congregational number. This is the best account I can offer for the seemingly ever-expanding Christianity of this nation. I am left to wonder, however, as man of the Christian faith, if the effects of being subject to the free market produce the genuine and committed Christian of times previous of this nation and the quality required for the revitalization and revival of this nation and Western civilization now and in the future. It must be said that the invisible hand can do a great deal but it will struggle to ensure the indispensable foundation of a genuinely ethical polity, which is where this land is unique in its religious character and in being a state that has promoted liberty.

A Product of His Environment

Religion is known to buttress the morale, confidence and unity of any community, and the man of this country most certainly appears to have harvested most fruitfully. The American is the most confident and articulate of men, although he finds such an assertion most surprising. I cannot help but marvel at the verbal expression and presentation skill of even the most impoverished and uneducated men of this land. After close examination of the American, I can settle only on few explanations of his exceptional confidence and eloquence, one of which rests with the immersion of Christianity in his culture. While it clearly is a combined product of culture including education, patriotism and democratic interest, the religious element of this package, the outsider surmises, is undervalued. This should occasion no surprise as the modern English tongue was born in the minds of Wycliffe and Tyndale as they set about translating the inaccessible Latin scriptures into the common speech of England. But it is when the visitor joins the American in the pews of his churches and is greeted with the educated zeal and verbal artistry of preachers, shaping words to sharpen minds, revive spirits, uplift the downcast and relieve the vulnerable, that he truly appreciates its effect. It is my presumption that this heightened language floats in the subconscious of the American, and consorts with the assuredness delivered by his faith, to generate coherence of an almost expressive quality. The essential ingredients of effective speech are self-belief and confidence, and in the culture of this land, it appears most definitively the case that religion facilitates such context. With only few notable exceptions countable on the one hand, this country has produced the greatest and most inspirational orators of the modern world; a predicament most owing to the persistent Christianity of this man.

It is not that I have been unaware that all theology is political; in fact, I have known it for some time as a serious Christian, yet here it is in a most amplified form that I barely recognize. This man's faith and values are inseparable; faith and politics fused. It is in this nation, most common for the church to combine its religious view with social and political action, an indication of the freedom without consequence here; there exist entire networks of publication across the multiple mediums of radio, television, print and electronic. The spirit of independence requires self-control; temptations of the flesh subvert such spirit; these are matters incumbent on the parents of children to offer protection.

I am called to the observations of Alexis de Tocqueville, the famous French thinker of more than two centuries ago, as I sort these matters in my mind:

> Upon my arrival in America, the religious aspect of the country was the first thing that struck my attention, and the longer I stayed there the more I did perceive the great political consequences resulting from this state of things, to which I was unaccustomed.

But de Tocqueville went further, noting what the outsider today still discerns of the American; the correlation of Christianity and the virtue of freedom:

> The Americans combine the notions of religion and liberty so intimately in their minds that it is impossible to make them conceive of one without the other.

Where the man of other lands perceives religion as limiting to his and others' individual freedom, the American produces a national amalgam. The rock, mortar and marble of American history, much of it in his capital reads the same as the American's mind: that the Creator is the source of American liberty, and that God's sovereignty resolves that all human authority is delegated. Put another way, and perhaps more simply, the man of this land believes that his fundamental rights come from God, and are therefore inalienable.

The later de Tocqueville observation of the American holding his faith as "indispensable to the maintenance of Republican institutions" and a topmost source of his democracy, I have concluded, also remains brilliantly accurate. The man of this land speaks with utter conviction for the requirement of religion in his democratic society. His genius is in his individual enterprise of Christian self-government; the greatest of his many products and exports. The man here is the most self-governing I have encountered; even if he has lost his way, he is loath to seek assistance, preferring to struggle through. While he remains at all times optimistic, I find him to be most accepting of the view of the sin nature of man, the same his founders shared; not in the least surprising given the Christian nature of such view and the faith of those holding it. But it is the extension of this view and its consequence that make the man here exceptional: he sees self-government as the only prevention of corruption and tyranny. The visitor realizes in the flash of an instant that this is why the man here is so committed to the government of great limit in ambit and power.

A Man of Morals

It is clear to the visitor here that this self-determination of the Christian faith has created in this land a culture of morality and generosity. I find the man here irrefutably charitable; he possesses, largely, a heart of humanitarianism and pulse of philanthropy. He is far more inclined, than any man I can think of, to part with whatever of his money he can afford, if it is in aid of charity. The individual charity of this land truly staggers; I have witnessed even the poor widowed lady of most senior age donate one of her most precious dollar bills to the philanthropic cause. The visitor, without statistical survey, can rely only on his observation but comfortably estimates that for each man of another country, the American would at least treble his contribution. The man here incontestably favors church and community in the provision of social welfare to his government. Given the size and role of his government, although it grows alarmingly and unnecessarily, it is imperative that the man here care for his American brother or sister.

The men of other lands are, in matters of the humanitarian, by the size of their government, abrogated from individual responsibility; worse, such circumstances can only eliminate altruism, conditioning selfishness. It is not that the man here is born better, I realize, but that his structures of government and their resulting cultural influence form a far superior human. The visitor is convinced by the man he finds here, and his observations; finding proof that the larger the government is, the worse the citizen becomes.

I observe also that denominational and theological difference pencils only a feint line among the religiously observant Christian American, with minimal difference in civic and private outcome. The man here talks of his denominational change casually but excitedly, citing eloquently his justification, and detailing his personal experience. In the south of this land is the home of the evangelical, although his mindset resides in most men here; he is a man who emphasizes the teachings and authority of the Scriptures in opposition to the institutional authority of the church itself. It is, of course, no revelation that evangelism is in the religious character of this man; it was precisely this that separated the first of his ancestors from the customary Roman Catholic philosophy of his era. The American of today remains, it would seem, committed to the belief in the personal and direct relationship of the individual with God, without intermediary, most in line with the Calvinist tradition.

Considering the orthodoxy of the evangelical mentality here and in this man, I again am struck at the natural ease with which the pieces of the complex American jigsaw fit; evangelism, or its practice, a manifestation of the intersection of individualism and Christianity. It does seem that the men of this land can repel with success the perilous counterculture; at the very least, it must be said that the visitor finds little evidence of any lasting effect of the sexually libertine era of the Sixties. I think it most reasonable to assume that it was the evangelical mentality of the man here that insulated his faith during these trials. The American is quick to boast that his Christianity grew during this period, and again, I am left to marvel at his adaptability to navigate the right course, most similar to a boomerang.

For all the clear staying power of religion in this land and its innumerable churches, matters of faith are surprisingly fluid. While some inherit their congregation or faith, it is most common for the American in his lifetime to change his denomination, or switch his church or congregation membership more than once; a symbol of the continual American footrace in self-improvement and reaching the finishing line of his dream and objectives. The visitor finds uncommon in this countryman of once scant religious fervor that is "saved," choosing to pivot his body stance in the direction of God, a sign of his movement away from his past, and the ills of it. The American, when recounting his decision to the outsider to embrace the church and God, speaks solemnly, in quiet tones as he recounts the trauma of his past, and reflects on the changes sustained since his former life ended. As he moves on to his current life, his volume increases and his tone gains variance; his speech radiant in enthusiasm and projecting in optimism.

No man visiting this land can escape the feeling that the faith of this man has further inculcated and nurtured his already existing sense of "chosenness," a most fundamental tenet of his culture. It offers his unique founding further substantiation and frames his overarching narrative with easy compatibility. The American has faith in a provident God and believes God was an active agent in American history. I am most moved by perhaps this man's most powerful image of history: his first President, George Washington, on his knees in the snow at Valley Forge; the words of Abraham Lincoln echoing the sentiment of this man:

> I have been driven many times to my knees by the overwhelming conviction that I had nowhere else to go.

For all the military might at this man's disposal, I realize it is this man's steadfast belief that his country serves a providential purpose that is his greatest weapon. While many here exhibit uncharacteristic coyness on this specific matter, I suspect most strongly that inside him the belief resides that God is neither neutral or indifferent to his nation; that his country is at least favored, at best chosen, with a divine mandate. This dualistic perspective, devoid of nuance, and most compatible with what I have witnessed of the American, would be to many outside this land obnoxious and loathsome. It is this assertion which drives and frames

Exceptional America

the civil religion of this country. Only such an in-built conviction can account for the nature of his history; one rich with this sentiment, from the suggestion of Benjamin Franklin for the Great Seal to portray Moses parting the Red Sea to the declaration of John Adams that the early settlers of America were "a grand scheme in Providence."

It must be said that history is on the side of the man here believing most unfalteringly in national providence. The visitor that reads General Washington's November 1781 letter to the President of Congress, acknowledging the numerous providential events of the Revolutionary War, or about the battle of Monongahela in which a young George Washington appeared "bulletproof" spending two hours with his life in the balance are difficult, even for the outsider, to construe other than God's providential care of America.

He Stands with Israel

I am curious to learn that the man of this giant nation is harbors a great love for Israel, a tiny country in the sea of the Middle East. He speaks of the admittedly august nation with great veneration in the most similar style to which he would speak of his own nation. It is true that the nation of Israel is most worthy of admiration and support, even love; it is an unfaltering democracy and a clarion call for excellence and peace. But it is, on the surface, unusual for the man of this nation to speak of the men of others at all, let alone in such laudatory terms. But as the visitor comes to realize; this nation is incorrigibly linked to the state of Israel in the most numerous of ways. This is not to say that this land has been in the past without the putrid stain of anti-Semitism; it is to say that the distinctive synthesis of Christian faith, politics and patriotism presiding in this nation is unequivocal in outcome: Israel is an American value.

There appears a unique nexus between the man here for Israel that is also for America and faith. I am hit with the realization, as I probe these matters internally, that the American conflates his own exceptionalism with that of the Israeli. This is a most logical connection given Israel's democratic existence amid perpetual adversity and record of academic, scientific and technological success. But the outsider feels the connection does not end nor is powered chiefly by this logic; rather that it rests with the Christianity of the American.

I am left to make the hypothesis that the man of this land, both understandably and rightfully, finds both political and religious resonance in the providential story of Israel. It is clear that the mind and religious character of the American interprets the events of the Israel narrative as a further pellucid indication that the content of the Bible can be trusted. I see the logic in this religious position; it is beyond remarkable that two thousand years of Jewish oppression and statelessness could be followed by not only their restoration to the Holy Land but also the creation of a deeply successful and democratic state. The American's knowledge of the word of the Bible means he understands piercingly, his obligations to the Israel state and the consequences of abandoning them.

Yet the visitor also identifies a political connection between this land and Israel. There is a distinct confluence between each man's values and cultural conservatism. Both the men of these countries are naturally disposed to patriotic sentiment and fierce desire for sovereignty; contrary to the objectives of the internationalist or supra-nationalist agenda to transcend borders.

If the man of America continues to uniquely comprehend the simple equation that virtue cannot be sustained in the absence of Christianity; and that if virtue is absent, then liberty must be as well, I see few ways the men of other nations can catch him. His adherence to this equation is his security of exceptionalism. As de Tocqueville noted: "Despotism may govern without faith, but liberty cannot." The other words that many of the men here appear to live by, and in my view, must continue to subscribe to ensure his exceptional state are those of the great President Ronald Reagan: "If we forget we are One Nation under God, we will be a nation gone under."

Chapter 4
GOD'S TROOPS

The fight against evil can only be categorized as the noblest act of the human, and success of that objective, his greatest achievement. It must, therefore, stand to reason that the noblest cause and greatest accomplishment of any nation is the same struggle. And it cannot be denied that the land I find myself in has dedicated itself more to this fight than any other.

The history of the modern world, when taught factually, without bias and with balance, affirms to any of its students the debt of gratitude owed to the man of this land. Without him, it must be said the lands of Europe would suffer under tyranny, the Asian continent under the dictate of a single Emperor, the nations of Australia and New Zealand under the control of the Japanese and the people of Eastern Europe without a taste of the freedom the men there today have. The American is understandably most proud of his victories and maintains resolutely, and I have no reason to not agree with him; the magnitude of these accomplishments spared an almost certain descent of a new Dark Ages upon the man of everywhere.

I cannot doubt, as I am here, that the exceptionalism of this man's military is the greatest manifestation of his

Exceptional America

land's exceptionalism. I discover early in my travels that the man here considers evil a noun, not an adjective. He holds, and it is the product of his civil religion and personal faith, a dualistic, unambiguous and black-and-white worldview that colors him and the decisions his leaders make. He is animated in any elucidation of this view, and the visitor is suddenly aware when observing his eyes that it is precisely this that has lead the American to be the first of men to boldly step forward to put an end to savage marauding of freedom. The man here appears to never choose the sideline; always the frontline in these matters, indeed, almost every matter, such is his nature. I am left to consider the standing of his military as the finest of the world as greatly owing to this conspicuously gallant panorama.

It is certainly true that at the core of any great nation a strong military must lay but the true test of the greatness of a polity is the cultural weight it lends to its troops. The man here has a visceral, unconditional love of his armed forces; much like the one a mother has for her child. It is a worship of equivalent level to that which he has for the matters of the patriotic and religious; indeed, the visitor finds great evidence that the American melts the latter two with the former: he believes that his troops are God's, carrying out His work. The visitor finds that this love and appreciation of things military is far in excess of that of any other man. Where the men of other countries generally greet their respective militaries with courtesy and platitude, the man of this nation has an incomparable reverence and adulation. The man here appears to understand better than any the reality that the few men that stand tall are the reason that some in society can stand at all. There seems, to the outsider here, not an American untouched by the military in their lives.

Nick Adams

Fervent Support of the Military

It is not uncommon here in this land, that feels often like a world, to see the American in the public place wave, salute or signal approval to the men or women of uniform. In fact, and I have witnessed on more than occasion, man here approaches the man of uniform, and politely interrupt him to express his gratitude for his service. But I have never been left more breathless, or ever felt such overwhelming clarity of this man's exceptionalism, than the morning I saw an ovation given by him to whom were either homecoming or outward-bound military personnel in the airport. Each American around me instinctively stood to wildly applaud and loudly cheer until this small band of intrepid freedom fighters were no longer in sight, although clearly always in his mind. But this man's affection for his military never ceases to surprise the outsider, nor its public display. The visitor surprises also at the sheer number of mothers that he hears of, or meets, that have now or in the past temporarily left their husband and children to deploy in patriotic duty, a most powerful and exceptional commitment that I can only admire.

There is in this land, as I have noted earlier and appears most clear, a most profound militarism; one that sets him apart from his Western cousins, even those with the English tongue; the most striking difference perhaps his gallant Australian ally: a martial people if pushed, but never militaristic. It is clear to me that the man here sees his military as the protector and purveyor of freedom, and it must not be forgotten that freedom is his identity; it is what he first came to these shores for. As I travel the length and breadth of this nation, this man has set up extraordinary amounts of museums, memorials, artifacts, tributes and military cemeteries; a product of not just the grand virtue of militarism but also a masterful method by which to remind a citizenry of its service. It is, for all these reasons, why the military is such an integral part of the life of this man, and central to the impregnable fortress that is his mind: confidence, faith, passion and gratitude. I am struck when the veteran of this land recounts to me his visit to the local veteran cemetery with his wife to make funeral and burial arrangements; he asks the charge of two spaces, and is told he has already paid for it.

The love and passion for and of military by man is no less natural than that which he has for his nation. I consider any man resolute to the point of combative and aggressive in the defense of his values or land's interest to be of most sound psychological and cultural health. The American is a man of such individual and collective mindset, and such penchant for the natural once more reinforces to the outsider how unsullied the natural state of man in this land remains. This is made all the more impressive, in light of the sustained social reinvention efforts of the elite of all manner and their ambition to relativize and feminize, in similar method to their wars on individuality, patriotism and religion, both in this land and in others. Again the unmodified nature of the man here unwittingly taunts the elite, and is further rubbed in by his unique expression. One can only imagine the looks on the faces of such elites were they met with the American's Armed Forces Recruitment Centre in the very center of Times Square in New York City; an equivalent embodiment of such bold superiority in the major cities of any other nation culturally inconceivable, but also impossible.

Nick Adams

A Strong Defender of Human Rights

I discern in this man a fierce demand for his human rights, albeit in an extremely different and unrecognizable form to which I, and presumably other outsiders, are accustomed. Where the outsider is inclined to gain the consensus of the world before commencing military action; the American believes, most rightly it must be said, the morality of protecting his liberty from the unwelcome intrusion of foreign bodies. It is in this way he is demanding of his human rights; his vehement belief in the sovereignty of his nation is reinforced by his own overpowering individualism; his mind endows his land with her own individualism among world lands. And so, I must conclude that the American nation is a living embodiment of the primary virtue of her people. This matter is hardly in isolation; it is accompanied by muscular faith, values and masculinity, all of which predispose this man to the unilateral act. It can be stated no more simply: this is a man that is reluctant to rely on the goodwill of the world; he is self-determining. In this way, the teeth of the American form a most stark contrast to the limp wrist of the foreign body. The man here aspires to lead; the outsider wears a badge of hesitation and failure, largely a result, I feel, of his insistent advance or tacit approval of bureaucratic internationalism. The international organization, the impotent brainchild of the relativist and internationalist, it must be said, suffers an inherent weakness, and is striking only its capacity for moral destitution. I find this to be the great moral and political difference of this land to others; the outsider in the last half century has demonstrated a deficiency in fighting evil, a seeming consequence of the alarming dearth of moral clarity in his land. Where the man here is undoubtedly committed to the fight against evil in the world; the outsider is largely unfocused on it, more energized and passionate about matters of environmental protection.

It is clear that at the heart of the American lies the strong virtue of service. The visitor learns quickly that the man of the United States Armed Forces, be it in the Army, Navy, Marine Corps, Air Force or Coast Guard is equally probable to hail from the big city as he is from the town so small it does not appear on the visitor's map. These American men of this superb creed have been in consistent war in the twentieth century, and permanently in the twenty-first. I cannot help but feel that this continued participation has had the effects of increased patriotism, fortified morale, and bolstered unity on this culture. And again, in the face of this, I am left to determine whether it is providence or supreme exceptionalism, or perhaps an amalgamation of the two, that leads to this; it is well-known in the history of man that war devastates and incurs a loss of time to every nation, except this one. The sluggish here is replaced by the flourish; even the economy of this man appears to be benefited by war, with many outside men convinced that the severity of the Great Depression may not have been what it was had it not been for his delayed involvement. It is also not lost on me that this nation is clearly blessed in her geography; with Canada to her north and Mexico to her South, the American knows there is remote chance of military attack from his neighbors. Almost uniquely, this man has not fought a war with one of his neighbors in over a century, allowing him to focus his efforts elsewhere.

But my observations are not to extol war; the human tragedy and cost far offsetting any level of cultural compensation. The man here, the visitor finds is unequivocal in his support of action to liberate societies, eliminate threats, and set other lands in a new and improved direction. The price of spreading his virtues to the corners of the world has been enormous, and stirs the deepest reaches of the American soul. The emotion of this man, in discussing military service and the fallen, bubbles to the surface, irrepressible, with many a moistened eye. The Arlington Cemetery in this land's capital is at once sobering and impressive; an aesthetic delight extraordinary in size designed for public and private tribute. I am heart wrenched at the sight of the middle-aged American with only a flimsy fold out chair, sobbing uncontrollably while visiting a lost son. Such observations are common in this land, and remind the outsider and American here alike of the price of spreading freedom.

Once here it is easy for the visitor to understand why the military of this nation is the target of the anti-American; it is his purest and most tangible manifestation of exceptionalism. It appears that the inequality of American military power grates on the jealous outsider, often spawning the unwarranted castigation and intentional smearing of the serviceman here. But it is seldom recognized that the American has only ever deployed in response to aggression, not to cause it. Notwithstanding his supreme military capability, his force has only even been moderate or measured; the American quick to point out his response to the unprecedented scale and nature of the September 11 attacks as an example of such restraint. It is true, also, that the military uniform of this man is to the free eye of the oppressed civilian as the oasis is to the man without water; he runs to it, not away from it and there are few uniforms of history that boast this effect.

I find it most fitting that the value-centric American has transformed necessary wars of self-defense into campaigns of spreading positive values for it indicates what I consider, the great misunderstanding of this man by the outsider. The man here bristles, rightfully, at the charge he has entered war territory or treasure or oil; to believe this is to not understand the American's values or mind set. To the man of this land, his mind and values meet to produce a moral reason for each occasion his country has committed itself to war. The irony of the foreign detractor interpreting of the pursuits of war and America as suggestive of a morally bereft society is therefore clear, but more aptly, preposterous; I challenge any visitor to this land to prove in observation or feeling the charge of moral impoverishment. While it is true that there is no other man on this earth that possesses such sets of mind or ideals, there also exists no other nation such as this in mankind's history. It surprises little that men of other lands feminized by secularity, big government, and relativism, with all its soullessness, considers any act of aggression greatly abhorrent. It is, with further irony, the words of another outsider, the famed British philosopher named John Stuart Mill that best encapsulates these sentiments: "War is an ugly thing, but not the ugliest of things. The decayed and degraded state of moral and patriotic feeling that thinks nothing worth a war is worse." A nation such as this one can never be loved; in any event, the man here, I assess, is not most benefited by affection, and therefore should not expend energy toward this end. A respected or feared nation is a commodity of much greater advantage to this man, and in the case of this his land, a benefit to mankind.

Bravery Unmatched

Many have described the man here as insolent; this may well be in some instances true but I see little reason to condemn this trait for I see in this man that his insolence in peace translates to his bravery in war. It was, of course, his insolence that ensured the commencement of his experiment; he should lose this only at his own peril. But it converse that the military in this nation, an employer of a scale most unimaginable, tunes the insolence of the young man with variable education and background, endowing him with discipline and integrity. The man here is most protective of this employment and any cuts to the military from the budget. When the outsider is fortunate enough to visit a base or one of the public military colleges of this nation, it feels as if it is its own world with facilities one marvels at. It is through this that the American enables many young men to achieve their dream. I cannot help but feel that the military of this nation is most integral and to tinker with it, its opportunities, size, or spending would be most unwise as it would, not least of all, radically alter the career paths of many young men and women.

There is in the military of this nation a necessary ruthless streak, not unique in the context of war but at first glance, incompatible with the morality and, at times infuriating, consistency of the American character. The man here has raised the ire of some ordinary men and women of other lands for his detainment facility of Guantanamo Bay and its practices of waterboarding and certain interrogative techniques; many who regard these as unpalatable and indefensible, but more critically, hypocrisy. The outsider outrages at the inconsistency of the invasion of another country on moral grounds and the absence of its equivalent in these acts. But while I am forced to accept the prima facie breach of the values, freedom and Christianity that define this man, I am unable to reconcile them with what is now fixed permanently in my mind: a moral justification, right or wrong, agreeable or otherwise, exists behind his every act. And I must say, I do have reason to see the morality in such actions. I, and quite clearly the American, as a man of principle, do not see the adoption of required action to protect a national citizenry from mass acts of terrorism a violation of its moral values. If we are to accept that our lands are a safer place solely because of the man here, then surely it follows that no greater morality can exist than ensuring this nation remain strong. The man here believes, and I cannot disagree that a choice between civilized restraint and Western survival is no choice; such a threat must be met with little hesitation. The American may be alone today in such thinking but he is hardly unique in the context of history; the logical view of war as war and a place for no compromise shared by many. I am reminded of Winston Churchill, the great wartime Prime Minister of England, and his demonstration of such sentiments throughout the Second World War, with the bombing the German city of Lübeck purely to damage German morale, planning to mustard gas any German invasion, and ignoring the hunger strike of Mahatma Gandhi in 1943. It is my estimation that the conscience of the man here would be more greatly affected by the morality of the potential consequences of Western collapse or weakness than the individual human rights of the enemy combatant.

I am amazed at the role of the military in securing the man here unprecedented reach and power, physical and economic; controlling the air, seas and outer space. The chasm in military might between this land and others must be extraordinary; I cannot imagine the rest of the militaries of every other man combined a match for the American. While it is true that the man here, by virtue of his militarism, has augmented the size and power of his military with unparalleled spending, this is by no means the only reason for its unprecedented scope: never has there been a military with a greater tactical or sagacious mind. It has enhanced immeasurably the lives of the man and outsider alike, through development and innovation producing e-mail, internet and the global positioning; not forgetting its advancement of scientific and technological research. This leadership of this man's military is substantial; it has furthered the human of every stripe, color and creed and I nor even the man of such great mind as the American could imagine the world of today without these leaps. The military man of this country, I am assured, strives, seeks, finds and never yields, and I am inclined to believe this as I note these attitudes in the American industry, much of which I find are led by men of past military service. As I search for the footholds of this man's ingenuity, I am struck by the military kinship of each that I determine: acumen, aggression, core discipline, lateral thinking and mental strength. I am left with no other conclusion to draw: the renowned strategy, prescience, efficiency, and diligence of this man is beholden to the example set by his fellow man in the most patriotic duty.

The military of the man here serves to not only protect and defend him and his allies; it protects every man of every land, standing ready at all times to deploy, engage and destroy. When it is put to the man here that his nation epitomizes a selfish and imperial foreign policy for purely analytical purpose, his back stiffens, and he is almost impudent when he declares that it is only due to him that the any man walks free. It is known that this land has, for at least its last fifty years, beginning with the European Recovery Act, or so-called Marshall Plan, effectively cross-subsidized the defense spending of many lands, including those of

Exceptional America

the European and Australian, and furnished each with stewardship of extraordinary sweep. Having been spared the financial burden of national military defense, the men of many of these countries have been the recipients of generous welfare programs by their government, to ensure their re-election. It is in this light that I find myself sympathizing greatly with this man's indignation; his generosity often reaching the hands of the anti-American minorities, and their preachers and organizers of hate within various lands. That is to say, the bloated welfare system of the West he fosters is the greatest enabler of modern day Islamic terrorism; it is a most wretched truth; and one for which I cannot see an easy solution. This is the first time I note an unforeseen jarring in this man's plans and thinking; the customary experience of all matters coming together appear to desert him here.

I had, prior to coming here, heard only from the outsider that had served alongside the American infantryman, and it must be said, all without exception spoke with veneration of the practices and code of the great American military. Being here I can now better understand their claims that that this man, in war is relatively unrestrained by paperwork or regulation; a situation that clearly prospering of confidence, clarity and aggression in the sensory overload of battle, and the ability to impart inspiration to fellow soldiers. It has been confided in me by the soldier of the mother country that even when armed to the teeth, he feels only genuine security upon the American's presence. I had heard of the famous American Marine, a reportedly fearless man of uncommon valor. When you meet him, he may look ordinary but there is something in this man's eye, even long after he has worn the uniform, that convinces he will freeze the sweat and chill the bones of the man with dreams of tyranny. The emblem and Latin motto of this man could not be more fitting to his mission, the former comprising the eagle, globe and anchor and the latter culturally abbreviated to *Semper Fi*, a reference of the most dear significance to every man that walks this land.

With the Marine of the exceptionalism that he is, I can offer few words on this paper to accurately reflect the Navy SEAL of the Special Forces Command. He is the most elite of the American man; a man of the rarest talent, dripping with courage. If the man of this land were to have a face of inspiration, it is him. His mind, I find to be the most powerful of any man anywhere; it is a unique confederation of strength, individualism, faith, patriotism and eternal optimism. As I read the opening and central paragraphs of his official philosophy, expressed with the inspirational rhetoric I have come to expect of any man here, I feel the hairs of my back stand. The power of his words equally affect the American and the visitor; such is his way:

> In times of uncertainty there is a special breed of warrior ready to answer our Nation's call; a common man with uncommon desire to succeed. Forged by adversity, he stands alongside America's finest special operations forces to serve his country and the American people, and to protect their way of life. I am that man.
>
> I will never quit. I persevere and thrive on adversity. My Nation expects me to be physically harder and mentally stronger than my enemies. If knocked down, I will get back up, every time. I will draw on every remaining ounce of strength to protect my teammates and to accomplish our mission. I am never out of the fight.

The general man of this land is of intuitive understanding that the belief in him of others can only follow his own self-belief, again underlining this man's penchant for the nature of logic. I find it clear that for as long as this man is the provider of belief in himself, failure is rendered an impossible outcome. While it is true these words bear the carriage of special contextual resonance, I have little doubt they are chiseled in the stone mind of every man as he travels his Maker's plan; for the man without it, he must gain it for it is the syrup of his lasting success.

First Responders

The man here is more acute in his awareness than any of his contemporaries that with great power arrives great responsibility; an awareness that once couple with his values is most substantial and invaluable in matters of the humanitarian. The military of this country is the primary vehicle of this work, I discover, as I travel through speaking to a great number of men and women. I am surprised to learn this not because I consider this man unlikely for such a role; to the contrary, he is ideally suited; but because it is the most overlooked and barely acknowledged aspect of this man's military. This, however, does not surprise, given that it most often is the anti-American behind the world camera, focusing the lens on other matters with great success.

Food, clothes, shelter, and essential supplies are delivered through the successful implementation of programs, reliant on the resources of this man's military; a financial and physical scope of aid unrivaled. He is instrumental in his response to the international disaster; such humanitarian effort easy to identify: the cataclysms of Haiti, Indonesia, and Iran in the last decade. Here, once more, this man shows his admirable character, providing assistance to nations, many of whose citizens daily pray for America's downfall; a most incompatible reality with the assertions of an immoral nation by the anti-American collective.

He is also the first of any man to respond to the tragedy of the outside. He is best placed to assist with his exceptional equipment and technology, able to assist in ways no other man can. In recent times, the American was the first to respond to the worst aviation accident in French history, in which two hundred and twenty eight perished, on the national French carrier. The men of France immediately requested of the American to use his satellite equipment to locate the aircraft and any bodies and he did, deploying his military personnel, maritime surveillance and patrol aircraft, to participate in the search and rescue effort. I raise this matter only in that the Frenchman is today the most vocal anti-American of the West, and yet the American soul, a product of virtue and faith, prevailed. The unequalled efforts of the American in Acquired Immune Deficiency Syndrome (AIDS) assistance in Africa is further substantiation, of what I and many of those outside visitors before me, identify as goodness.

I find the American uncharacteristically quiet on all matters of philanthropy and humanitarianism; he seems intent on receiving scant recognition in what I can only deem a correspondence to biblical instruction that charity never desires or seeks its own praise, or honor or profit, or pleasure.

The man of this land exhibits a greater mindfulness of freedom as a most perishable gift than any other I have known, which is clearly to account for his freedom lasting over two hundred years, a most unknown phenomena in history. But this consciousness has the propensity to slowly fade, and while it is hard to identify as this man is such a great deal freer, there is a slight shift to be observed at this time. It feels that only a most sustained vigilance can see the improbable experiment of this man continue, to ensure his Republic; only the replication of the valiant valor exemplified by his military on the home front will be sufficient for his survival. But it is again the prescient planning of the American, most reminiscent of his founders, that fills me with deep hope and suggests this land may yet be at the peak of its power. This man knows that his young must possess the identical zeal for freedom and takes independent action, outside of the unreliable classroom. The visitor enthuses and fascinates at the countless character-building institutions of the American for his children; instilling of leadership, courage, self-confidence, ethical behavior, and sportsmanship. These uniquely patriotic establishments of America teach the young men and women of this land the essential survival skills of shooting and hunting, furnish relationships with mentors and condition him to competition early. It is these institutions that water the earth of American exceptionalism, making it bear and sprout.

The words of the famous American, General Douglas MacArthur, that rung in the ears of the cadets of the exceptional West Point, must have renewed sound for the fatigued man of this nation, in whatever form his service takes:

> The long gray line has never failed us. Were you to do so, a million ghosts in olive drab, in brown khaki, in blue and gray, would rise from their white crosses, thundering those magic words: Duty, Honor, Country.

This does not mean that you are warmongers. On the contrary, the soldier above all other people prays for peace, for he must suffer and bear the deepest wounds and scars of war. But always in our ears ring the ominous words of Plato, that wisest of all philosophers: "Only the dead have seen the end of war."

Chapter 5
EXCEPTIONAL AND INDISPENSABLE

The culture of the American swims with exceptionalism; open, buoyant, bold and exciting; it is, it has to be said, without peer. Success and audacity reside in the heart and soul of the man here; he thumbs his nose at the vanilla and pedestrian. He reserves his greatest disdain for not the state of mediocrity but the aspiration to it. He lauds the eccentric, and celebrates with the greatest force of life the individual, at the expense of the collective. This is a land where fierce competition is sponsored and an entrepreneurial spirit breathed.

Strikingly, the culture of this great nation is possessed of an air of supreme confidence, inflating the American essence. It is a powerful machine capable of tremendous precision; working at its optimum, man fulfils his destiny, with the weak becoming strong and the strong becoming great. The national culture of the American has allowed him extraordinary domination, never before witnessed in the history of the man, and the man here is knowledgeable of this. The ages of the agricultural, industrial and information have belonged to him; human innovation translated to human inventive genius. The cultural exports of this land to the furthest corners of the world have no boundary, and her scientific discovery equally limitless. Economically, scientifically, militarily and culturally, the land I find here is grandly exceptional, with the man here setting the standard, and the outsider taking action with one eye firmly fixed on the American experience.

As I spend significant time here visiting this man's many counties, it is impossible to not notice the many extraordinary men, of distinguishing accent betraying their life as previous outsiders in leading industry roles, and with flourishing career. But while the flight of the talented and ambitious from their native lands to here is not novel, even diagnosed as the so-called brain drain, I hardly expected, before coming here, that this activity to be as eminently explainable to the outsider as it is. It is violently clear that the man here could not see matters more differently than the men of other lands. Where the outsider culture, armed with socialistic sympathies, views its best and brightest as a relaxed comfort, a demographic to which little or no responsibility is due; I observe that in this country their American equivalents are the most intentionally nurtured, mentored, guided, promoted, and rewarded. The talented and ambitious outsider makes this country his new home as his appetite for ambition is satiated only here; his dreams of greatness facilitated through opportunity.

The national culture of this land is, as I have said elsewhere, the construct of foundational events, stout Christianity and individualism. The man here emphatically underlines the individual in his appraisal of business, life, performance and social development; it appears that only on matters of national affairs does he focus collectively.

I find this to be converse to the outsider; a man arrested by the vague and undefined concept of teamwork, he is hostage to the development of character traits that qualify him a team player. Where collectivist doctrine stipulates no one individual be greater than any organization, such timid and weak insecurity finds no abode on this magnificent and fearless soil. The collectivist-minded corporate employer, for example, finds greater virtue in the individual bearing limited talent but team spirit, than the brilliant and strident individualist. Here in this, what still feels new, country the leeching, old world belief in the institution, prevalent in the English-speaking world and abounding in aristocratic overtures, is a diminutive influence. It is most often that the American will glorify the individual to the level where he or she replace the institution. I am drawn to the billboard advertisements adjoining highways and roads promoting a personal injury lawyer, employed by a law firm. These advertisements extol the abilities of the individual legal practitioner and suggest direct contact with him; conspicuously minimalist in their marketing of the firm. Such attention to the individual, unless by design of a sole trader or owner, is most unfamiliar to the outsider as it is scarce his culture.

From Many, One

The culture of this land, I find again, mathematical; the man here considers the individual operating at his optimum as elevating the collective, yielding the identical desired outcome of the collectivist, minus the diffidence. The primary difference, I am able to observe between this man and the non-American in reaching this objective is that the man here sees it accomplished naturally, wherein people are able to independently achieve without being subjected to the moral judgment and uneasiness about their role within a team. The capacity of this extraordinary man to dream must never be discounted, and the dream, much like the prayer, is an inherently personal act. Confiscating the dream of higher aspirations as the collectivist insists on is a most counterproductive act, furthering, in my mind, the case that the American has it right.

The man here is exceptional because his roots are profoundly anti-statist; sovereignty is invested in the people, not the state. When sovereignty rests with people, the capacity for human achievement is illimitable, as the American demonstrates. This is, as I deduce, the ultimate appeal of the American culture: it is a vehicle, motored by the liquid fuel of mainstay values, for the fulfillment of dreams through opportunity and risk. For a man that holds the rule of law in such esteem, I find that, when it is in conflict with matters of the heart or soul, he here is far more inclined to choose in favor of the visceral.

The man here is alternately dreaming and real, where paradox has been raised to an art form. There exists here a culture that I can only describe as the culture of yes; greatly unique, even to the Western outsider, closest in cultural matters, accustomed to a culture of "no." At the heart of a culture of "no" is the central attitude that consigns the people of that culture to obscurity. Leading pleasant and contented lives, characterized by conservative small steps, such cultures and their people have remote chance at bequeathing enduring legacy. The man here, I feel, has the correct view of life: that he is the music maker, the dreamer of dreams, and the only pursuit worthwhile is the seemingly impossible. The mindsets of negativity and mediocrity are most abnormal here, and in extremely short supply, a most pleasant environment. In this candid country, the dream is not merely an internal state of the mind but a verbal proclamation. Where the outsider, cloaked in secular humanist tradition, equates talk of hope and optimism with delusion and derides its proponents as excessive and discordant with reality, the man of this land greets any grand vision for individual life with enormous enthusiasm, and makes him feel the impossible to be possible. If I were to put in coarse terms: the Western outsider to this land belongs to a culture striving of mediocrity; the American is unabashed in his pursuit of greatness.

Healthy Competition

Any theoretical framework or reasonable hypothesis would suggest the propensity to dream would correspond with a society mired in unrealism. Yet the American, the greatest dreamer of men, resides in the country and culture closest to social Darwinism, a physical embodiment of reality. The man here, unlike the outsider, sees participation as unworthy of reward; there is no second place. Competition is everywhere across this great land, I find, and on every level; it is inescapable preparation for the real world. The children of this country are raised to understand the reality of competition and the emphasis on being the best. Pondering these matters, the visitor is struck at the difference of this upbringing to those generations of the young in other lands; the educator of other lands likely to inform his students at the conclusion of a sports game that despite the loss of one side, no winner existed, and that each player of both teams had won, a most delusional perspective.

Competition nurtures strong individual performance; when the individual performs at his best, there is a collective benefit. The man here is of an instinctive understanding that triumph on the world stage demands a native culture capable of accommodating internal competition. His drive to compete is fuelled by his correct conception of equality; the view that equality exists through natural law in the presence of individual inalienable rights. It takes the shortest of time for the visitor to this land to recognize that the experience of this man stipulates that the bleakness of a society must surely rest with the defective notions of equality; that it is a vehicle that drives the roads of egalitarianism to reach the destination of equal outcomes, bypassing the highway of competition and all its success exits.

The preponderance of the underdog in this culture I find to be matchless. The resonance of the underdog with the American dream of overcoming the circumstances of birth and achievement is most commanding. Where the outsider may be supportive of the underdog but conditions it on the success of the underdog and not his mere journey, the man here harbors a love with true legitimacy; he rewards courage and risk, immaterial of the outcome. The visitor is astounded by his observation that where the outsider may love a winner once he is victorious, the heart of the American is with the individual for his entire journey.

The infrastructure of this culture uses the cement of inspiration. I construe this signature characteristic of the American as also the bookbinder of the American story, responsible for his underdog appreciation, a partiality toward dreaming and the American dream itself. The visiting outsider cannot help but be stunned at the popularity and size of the self-help section of the American bookshop. It is a most common sight to see the man here engaged in reading the autobiography, or biography or receiving by other mode other forms of motivational material. The

American tunes his attention through reading, learning, watching and listening to those he admires the most, and attained the highest levels of success. I find this to be a most distinguishing element of human activity, and unique here in its frequency and range; the man here must surely be the most open of all men to self-improvement. This practice and predilection is entirely compatible with the exceptional love and celebration of the successful in this grand nation.

The rejuvenation of the human spirit is effected by inspiration; an inspired person is an emboldened one. I find that the man here is almost addicted to risk, boasting more chutzpah and audacity than the men of other nations. The man here again shows his federation of logic and nature, innately understanding that the need to be challenged is intrinsic to success; without risk, man cannot flourish. The culture that presides can only be described with the words encouraging, supportive and rewarding of the man willing to risk. Just as the great document of the American, The Declaration of Independence, is enshrining of his right to pursue happiness, the cultural attitude toward risk, it is revealed to the visiting outsider, affords a daily protection to this right across every inch of the territory of this enormous country.

Ever the Opportunist

I have already established that the American carries with him great emotion but I have perhaps not intoned sufficiently its entwining with the inspirational. Where man is predisposed to inspiration and dreams of a better life, he is equally infused with emotion. The response of the American to personal stories or triumphant journeys, in the wake of tremendous adversity, is fathomlessly acute. I find any audience within this country impulsive and unrestrained, generating energy in any room it finds itself. For the secular non-American, conditioned to aspire to mediocrity and value inconspicuousness, I imagine such outward display of emotion to be again excessive. Travelling through the spectacular mountain spine of this land, I am struck that it is the emotion and soul of this man that sources his nation's strength and global supremacy.

The inclusivity facet of the culture of this land is the root of the famous moniker "the land of opportunity" and the culture of yes that clearly exists. All over the lands of this world, men and nations alike have clambered upon the head of the American eagle, determined to share in his journey of opportunity. The man here ensures the requisite circumstances for true and inexhaustible opportunity by way of his welcoming nature. Where the outsider reacts first with skepticism and suspicion, I am amazed to learn the American is almost devoid of preconception and most accepting on face value. I find the man here places very little emphasis on a capacity to catch a man out, a great difference to the men of other lands. To the outsider, there is no greater feat or accomplishment than their ability to identify swindle or the disingenuous. To this end, he erects a protective wall; a wonderful defense mechanism for the honest few, but a bulwark impeding the opportunities of the many. In such societies, there exists no more apt example of the sentiment toward risk. The man in this culture is likely to subject all men to his protective wall, automatically greeting them with negativity and doubt, and at worst, total irreverence. This flagellating culture of the outsider erodes innovation, fostering an environment of reluctance where people consider insufficient benefit to such objectives. The man of this land implements an approach lacking in such narrowness, with far greater prescience; prepared to suffer the indignity of deception on occasion. It is for this reason that the seeds of much outsider innovation have been sown in international territories; yet the majority of such sees fruition in this land.

The American greets novelty and the eccentric with genuine inquisitiveness; most telling is the catch line of one cable giant in this land, capturing this national sentiment: "Characters welcome." The reward of an accessible and inclusive society is, to the American, an immeasurable advantage to both innovation and national disposition; he understands that is nothing is ventured, nothing is gained.

A Drive to Succeed

The American is a display of remarkable confidence, particularly in his judgment; I find the old-fashioned "vouch for" most alive in America. Where the outsider of the Western denomination exercises permanent caution, bearing the unconfident view that their opinion is only relative and may not be shared, the man here is most incautious. While such tendency might appear inconsequential, the contagiousness and permeation of inspiration and positivity must never be discounted as human glue. The man here is most averse to negativity, I find, equating it with learning to function in your dysfunction. The outsider's culture, coated with negativity, cultivates loud and effective carping from the sideline by those envious and bursting with disillusionment, to the detriment of the successful individual. The negative voice has little or no place in a positive culture, and is drowned or at least matched by rallying forces of support, and so it is most certainly the case here in America; this man loves the winner, and the state of success.

The collectivist media and political elites of the outsider country, fortified by cultures esteeming the undistinguished, consider entitled to a monopoly of judgment, with their views on acceptable modes of behavior or approach by the individual. The eccentric individual, challenging of the status quo and establishment, in these societies is judged a menace and pest, maladjusted to the team mindset. Independence, the promotion of one's self and individuality are the most feared qualities of man to the collectivist but in this land here and the man who inhabits it, and as in any society of the individual, they are indispensible to success and matters of ultimate personal virtue. Matters of eccentricity and innovation are a cause of fascination and celebration to the man here. He realizes the individual in the free collectivist nation, stymied and persecuted, bears semblance to the oppressed man living under tyranny. The true promise of opportunity is measured in availability; the American gives the greatest number of any nation his chance to succeed in the desire of his heart. The allusion to the "pursuit of happiness" is no guarantee of happiness; but the right to pursue it is assured. The visiting outsider finds the culture of the American enrobed in this right; opportunity is reliant upon freedom and this man, the freest of them all, offers it through his physical landmass, population number, and national exceptionalism.

The culture most visionary is the one, cognizant of the need for the achievement of generational transcendence, which earmarks the future generation for focus. The man of this nation, more than any other the visitor concluded, conceives the mentor to be the greatest agent in this mission, considered a patriotic duty. An innovation in American

Exceptional America

management, it must be said that the cyclical act of mentoring upcoming leaders is concurrently exceptional and inherently good. The outsider culture, emphatic in its lust for social equilibrium and reflective of decadent humanity, provides an infertile footing for the mentoring tradition; it must be said that self-interest and short-termism are the fruits of the secular society with the socialistic keystone. The American individual in this way takes ownership of his child's future; the outsider, as ever, absolves himself, hinging such responsibility on government. The outsider does not wish to endow the future generation with any support previously unforthcoming to him, yielding a cycle of permanent inertia and moral decay. The patriotic drought of the outsider serves as an exacerbation; a fragmented society has an aridity of national interest, with no outlook gaze to the future. This mentoring culture extends to academia, with the mentoring programs of the universities of this land unrivaled by even the best universities of the foreign land. The leaders of industry are more accessible, approachable and accommodating to the young aspirant, than any of their equivalents in other lands of the world; the American leader even known to respond to unsolicited communication. Such opportunity is scarce in the Western nations of the outsider; industry leaders meet industry aspirants only in the event that they belong to demographic groups whose interests the media or government promote as more significant than the whole society.

There must be unanimity among all visitors to this land: confidence seeps from the pore of the man here. His readiness to assert himself, coupled with his tremendous confidence, birthed by faith, patriotism and success, differentiates this man distinctly to the visitor. He, the most powerful of men, is also said to be the least humble of men. It should surprise few that any outsider, a product of the collectivist mentality, is inured to perceive confidence automatically as arrogance. Such a man's aversion to self-confidence is predictable; the inherently individual gearing of the virtue is unsympathetic to the cultural streetscape.

The man that speaks highly of himself and is active in his own promotion is most reviled in outsider cultures. Yet I find the man here considers these ventures as routine, entrepreneurial and essential to survival. The secular outsider cloaks his fear of the confident man with declarations of the virtue of humility, a reference of Biblical origin, an irony not lost on the man of this country. The American considers the counterfeit brand of humility espoused by the outsider as unbiblical, and the worst form of conceit. The culture with empathy for secular socialism does not accurately embody reality; the warm coddle of the ever-ready safety net a deterrent to exhaustive exertion and a purger of the instinctive survival edge. In the context of this confected environment, confidence, self-promotion and the aspiration to inspire the confidence of others in an individual's ability are rendered redundant.

I find that the man of this nation is the least envious of men and I can only reach the inescapable conclusion that it is his immense pride that prevents this envy. This presents yet another paradox of the man here; a deeply religious man, he is nonetheless most prideful. It is perhaps here that he exercises his most pragmatic element, sensing that rightful pride is an efficient and sufficient defense to envy, a state a stone's throw away from the stream of servility.

The American extends the ladder of opportunity only to the individual with sufficient self-belief; the absence of the government and dearth of collective mollycoddle means this man has no choice but to promote himself, in the knowledge that he has no other representation. The American is a man of humility, in his interpretation of life and events, guided by his faith: he knows, despite his self-determination, he is not in overall control. There is little evidence of replication in his career or social interaction; he has little choice in the matter, it must be remembered. I find the man here to view with distaste the dispassion and boredom said by his elites to accompany his needs; he understands his nation on an emotional level, ironically the deliverer of the measured response.

The Future of a Nation

The American child is the apple of the cultural eye. From the moment of his birth in this nation, he is administered greater freedom than his outside counterparts, prospering individuality. As the visitor observes the American parent interacting with their child in a public place, he finds it most revealing; a distinct emphasis on the child's self-expression overrides the parental instinct of behavioral boundaries. I find in this nation that these public encounters prime the child for individual public performance and instill supreme confidence. In my experience, I have found the outsider parent greatly uneager to similarly acquiesce their child, disposed to a collectivist message that their children should defer to social convention and be mindful of others by seeking scant attention. The five-year-old boy or girl of this nation is bountiful in confidence and most lucid; a strong contrast to his or her equivalent Western peers.

I can report a most interesting phenomenon that grows at great rate here in this far away land. The American child is increasingly the subject of home school, a prevalent method of education, and indicative of the man here's exceptional focus on his children. The outsider and American once more diverge here, and it is a steep divergence, and I find myself yet again siding with the man of this land. The outsider, it is undeniable, is today thoroughly ensconced in the discipline of government control of education, sadly convinced of the most unnatural: that the state is, and should be, the controller and shaper of a child's life and belief set. The American chisels in stone his contrarian belief, a most rightful one: that it is the parents of a child that bear ownership and responsibility for their child's general education. Homeschooling is the fundamental expression of individualism in education, and is therefore American to the core. Symbolizing an open culture with the choice for parents to either educate or engage the private tutor, it is available to all the economic classes of this country. The phenomenon of homeschooling finds itself still in seed form and has not yet been witnessed in full bloom; the latest pendant on the chain of this man's traditions that upholds individualism and self-determination.

The outsider balks at such a proposition; indeed in many of his lands, this practice is outlawed, such as in the European land and might of the German. It is a matter of fact, not presumption, that many families of the European have sought asylum here in this land as they have been persecuted for their desire to engage in such practice. The governments of the outsider wish to determine the manner and method in which the youth of their nation is trained; this land of the free upholds once more the natural, encouraging parents to decide the upbringing of their child. The governments of the outsider appear unmotivated by the welfare of the child, a motive that would perhaps be understandable even if misguided, but instead are driven by a tyrannical statist philosophical push to extinguish any parallel societies. The American man understands the consequential difference in the government raising the next generation, in place of individuals; a perfect illustration of the foreign lands holding government as the highest authority, and the American land holding the individual in its place.

Consumerism and Skepticism

This man here is an enormous consumer, undeterred by the substance of his consumption; he consumes with equal fervor a speech or media personality, as he does a product or brand. This consumerist culture, I find, is abetted by the dual existence of an absence of skepticism and energy for opportunity within this grand country. These are the enablers of the pursuit of happiness, or the dream that the American weds himself to; they are also liable for the wrongful outsider perception of this man to be of limited intellect and great ignorance.

It is true, I must concede, that the American consumes the media personality most deeply, with an almost religious fervor, convinced of their judgment, in light of their personal feats. These public displays of confidence feed the outsider's presuppositions of the American; a critical mind could never countenance such fervent worship. But it is clear to me as I have a moment of lucidness roaming someone in the breadbasket of this country that the disparity between the American and the outsider owes to the divergence on matters of success, emotion and aspiration. The man here sees his best chance in life as paramount, seeking a model of success of which to aspire. This occasions little surprise, for the culture most respectful and desiring of success, is here in this land. Emotion, hope, success-centrism, and optimism, the ingredients of the American success recipe, are misappropriated by the anti-American outsider to fallaciously cast aspersions on the intellect of the man here.

Indeed, there is a great degree of necessary skepticism in the American. He overwhelmingly favors his own judgment, seldom having faith in the expert opinion of others; I have only pity for the man that attempts to dictate to him. It is here that the American exercises skepticism; a better target than the aspiring entrepreneur, it must be said. This is not to say the American does not defer to professional judgment or respects the authority on a given matter; it simply is that his fierce sense of self-belief, the common man and distrust in the elites imbue him with a wary skepticism.

A Man of Opinions

The American is most opinionated; he would be best described an unbashful extrovert. The cancer of political correctness, I have found, is unable to metastasize on any significant level here in this country; moderation of opinion to spare offense is considered most weak and greatly diminishing of individuality. The mould of culture is set by an unquestionable unreservedness of personality. The state of self-confidence is most transmissible, and in this nation impressively mirrored in social interaction. Of all men, the American appears the most assured of his place, comforted by an abundant individual freedom and a belief in his sovereignty, traditionally the severer of the shackles of governmental oppression. I, the already speechless English-speaking outsider, accustomed to austere laws of libel and defamation, have my tongue further paralyzed when learning of the weakest defamation laws in the world existent in this land. It is true that the Western partners of the American do in their own nations officially declare the freedom of speech through law and right; but such proclamations are charlatanistic and disingenuous. Freedom of speech, in this country of America, is genuine; it carries not the delusory of the other nations. For in this land, man speaks his mind without fear of recrimination or dislodgement from society or career; the true test of freedom of speech, the moment where it fails to be suppositious. The society that allows man the freedom to speak his mind but punishes, ostracizes, dislodges, derides and traduces, with effect to employment and reputation, through authority and other opinion-forming bodies, devalues the greatest freedom of man with its illusive and spurious approach. It belts with considerable force the observing outsider that the American is the only man with authentic and indubitable guarantee to the freedom of speech; a state to which every nation should aspire.

The man here is often astounded to learn that in the countries of his English-speaking cousins, the citizen whose talents or achievement have distinguished him is resented, criticized, and targeted. The non-American culture is unforgiving and relentless to the successful individual, designed to eliminate confidence and superiority. The outsider desires a level society, as his statism is bone deep, even if unmindful. The statist, even if only of ankle-biting stature, detests personal success and is loath to allow it to be rewarded. These circumstances flourish mediocrity and failure, and offer nary incentive for achievement, inspiration or opportunity; it is in this society that success becomes a matter of personal shame. I feel it impossible for the American to be further from the outsider with statist proclivity; he replaces envy with deep admiration, respect and personal ambition. The greatest love of this man is the winner; success. Any visitor feels the power of breeding his culture engenders; to the contrary, he exerts every effort to assist success. There can be no doubt associated with it: this country is the greatest of any land for the successful individual.

Ingrained Philanthropy

The nature of the American is philanthropic, as I have already outlined; a feature starring in the economic and social prosperity of this nation. I find that in this land the homes and pocketbooks of the American are open to the needs of the elderly, handicapped and orphaned more so than any other man; a most commendable set of circumstances. The philanthropic blood courses through the cultural veins of the man here, first injected by the Christian faith, and manifested in the "Golden Age" with the great industrialists and bankers of this country such as men named Rockefeller and Vanderbilt and Mellon and Carnegie and Ford, and others. The visitor feels the palpability of such humanitarianism all across the nation; no surprise it is that the most generous philanthropists and their most enduring foundations are of American denomination. I find the patterns of the American's donation activity interesting; the man here appears to give with equal generosity to both the secular and religious cause. The structures of this man that preserve and emphasize his community, both democratic and cultural, are further significant allies of the noble practice of philanthropy. I find that the man here is again most forward thinking; he is most willing to help another man for he sees it as critical to defending his own independence; where help if offered cheerfully and without request in perpetuity, there is no feeling of debt or loss of dignity.

The American is a most articulate being; a fact that he is seemingly unable to recognize. Even the most impoverished man of limited education residing in the most undesirable parts of this vast land is most expressive and coherent, even eloquent. I must also make comment on the television culture here; it is pervasive in nature, assisted by population and market size and it exposes the child here to ceaseless high quality communication. The effects of such circumstances could suggest, alongside the religious character of this man, the explanations of such articulateness.

I must conclude after spending time here that the vociferous attack of the anti-American veiled in targeted criticism, is of an underlying nature aimed at the heartbeat of the culture of values that so clearly exists.

For as long as this country exercises fidelity to its blueprint of the Constitution and Declaration of Independence, thereby remaining true to her values, I find scarce evidence to suggest the reign of this man can be limited. The culture war is the ultimate ballgame of the soil of this stadium of freedom. The man here must remember that in the event of defeat, no other America or American exists as a savior; life as the Westerner has become accustomed to will also most surely perish.

Chapter 6

MERCANTILISM

The American conducts business in a manner most exceptional; his economic might is his upbearing pediment. It is, of course, most well-known that this most incredible country is the prime engine of all the economic growth and prosperity of the world. It is certainly true that the greatest accomplishment of any great nation is its ability to spread its culture and values to faraway lands and people, and the man here it must be said has achieved this without parallel; his businesses most pivotal to such objective. Business and employment in this land is upmost, occupying the highest echelons of this man's thought pyramid; it is through these that the American not only finds his worth but pursues his happiness and foments his famed opportunity. A consumer like this man has never been seen; he devours products and services with the thirst of the man stranded in the desert happening upon an oasis. I find this man's belief in wealth creation to be inebriating belief, and of the greatest fundamentality to the American experience.

No compliment is more august to this man than to offer him the label of entrepreneur. It is my opinion that entrepreneurial innovation is the currency most distinguishing of nations and fortunately for him these are values stenciled into the sheets of his history for generations; it should be mentioned they have no greater companion than this man's most prized documents: the Constitution and Declaration of Independence. As I spend time across this land, the visceral and visible conclusion I must draw is that it this innovation that often spares the American in crisis; it lifts the piano off his back.

Now that I have familiarized myself with this man and his faith, he believes most forthrightly that his challenges of this day will be the victories of the next; it surprises me not even slightly to learn that many of his most exceptional creations of business were born in the most economically inhospitable times. Many of the corporate giants of this land, familiar to the resident and outsider alike, are substantive proof: Microsoft, Hewlett-Packard, General Electric and IBM. These facts are most explicable: the absence of self-confidence inhibits creativity and risk, a deficiency the American does not suffer. He is a most self-confident man, and correspondingly creative and risk-prone. The visitor can only imagine that the proven ability of the American to be heard over the din at the world dinner table and his entrepreneurial blood are the materials of wealth dynamite, in this age of global and pervasive reach.

Service is an enormous priority of the business here; the indifference of other Western businesses toward it is foreign. The outsider cannot help but revel in delight at the attention he receives and the ebullience of the service employee he observes. No component of this man's economy is haler or more ingrained than the culture of performance; the longevity of its eminence means that the American no longer subjects it to analysis. It is to the outsider, at first, a most peculiar custom; fundamentally integrated into the economy here, almost automatic and virtually compulsory, is what the American refers to as the act of tipping. The outsider may be accustomed to making a rare exception in his land to truly outstanding service and the more affluent outsider perhaps with greater regularity; but in no country other than this is it as ingrained, irrespective of wealth of the customer. The employee of this nation, I find, relies on creativity to make ends meet, as this man has engineered his economy to offer low hourly rates.

It is the American's theory that the income of the employee of such work is uncapped; an enormous incentive to perform for individual reward. It therefore registers minimal surprise that the service offered in the private sector here is exceptional; the American employee typically greeting with a latitudinous smile and effervescent familiarity; he or she exerts considerable effort to be helpful, exude competence and provide the best experience to every man. To the outsider, this would be a most pleasant departure from what he is accustomed in equivalent arenas of his land. It is through this custom, too, I find, that the American cleverly demarcates the private and government sectors. The humanitarian spirit of this man flourishes in customary tipping; his values and Christian influence reinforced each time he provides a tip, reminded of the need to care for his fellow man in the community. Only this man, with his never-ending logic and surprise, could combine the humanitarian and spiritual with service and economy; a truly exceptional accompaniment embodying broader exceptionalism. This nation, a bastion of cultural conservatism, I find, is most charitable, signifying that the land embracing the leftist ideals is the least open-handed. I find the man here, for whom tipping is simply automatic, unlikely to fully appreciate these matters, evidence that perhaps he still lives on the foresight produce of men before him; an outsider with fresh eyes is perhaps more suited to appraise these matters and observe their exceptionalism.

Meaningful Work

The American believes in his vocation; he is always seeking a life of momentousness, of consequence, lucrative in meaning. This sentiment sets him importantly apart from the outsider who is a much more easily fulfilled man, with an eye to leisure and the arts. Employment gives man reason and definition; and the man here in his life audit considers his vocation with reverence, and welcomes its consequences for his role in society. He thrives on effort; without it, he meets an elephantine emptiness. It is through only his own human accomplishment that man can be genuinely contented, and the American's grasp of this is far superior to his contemporaries or generations of outsiders, again an example of his itch for nature. The personal pride of this man in his work, I find to be ever evident; it may waver somewhat in its consistency, but there is, I must say, there exists in him an approach most artisan. He appears to be most tilted in his work to the unique brilliance of the individualistic flamboyant.

It is said today in most mellow and placid tones across all borders, as if a long-established, accepted, and irrefragable fact that this country is the greatest on the earth to conduct business. Clear it is; this is the land favored most by the entrepreneur and business owner, including those of the outsider nations. The years of history record the healthy and flavorful marinade of capitalism, competition and innovation in this country; enormous effort expended in protecting the cardinal turbine of the economy: the entrepreneurial capacity of business. These flavors are the entrenched scoops of the American ice cream cone, and the values, when practiced with purity and without the intervention of government, with which he will continue to prosper, and that bathe his future with optimism. The man of other lands could not but help identify danger for the man here; the unprecedented accumulation of federal regulation asphyxiating the throat of the American business, in a chokehold most reminiscent of his lands.

I find that the climbing entrepreneur and self-starting businessman of other lands renew their dreams here, in the absence of cumbersome bureaucratic processes, cost-prohibitive matters and difficulty to attain capital, to which they are accustomed. The trade union is a most weak entity across the states of this land; unlike the other Western world, the employer and economy here most rarely find themselves held to ransom. These unique circumstances truly liberate the wings of the entrepreneur, I observe, speeding him through the inevitable winds of self-doubt and uncertainty that occasion in any event but are exacerbated by choking bureaucracy. The most essential capacity of man is to dream; without it, his mediocrity is foreordained; his resting place in the cemetery of commonplaceness assured. For the entrepreneur, the dream is similarly essential and non-negotiable, and the economic and cultural system of the man here, exceptionally understanding of human need, do not force him to depart the dreaming program for the maintenance program. The American man here, the master of optimism and self-drive, I find hardly lurches like the blind drunk in the dark alleyway every time he or his business or idea is the subject of criticism or ridicule; in fact, I note the face of the aspiring American, as all outsiders might; his stern gaze emitted in no small part by the intensity of his eyes.

Exceptional America

The man here, as I have said before, conceives competition like no other; it hypostatizes him, saturating his thinking. Competition is a natural circumstance of man, and a most beneficial one; once more I marvel at his steely resistance to the predominant, politically correct view of his Western counterparts: that, aside from organized professional sport, competition is morally questionable, as it promotes inequality. The exceptionalism of this gargantuan nation lies, I think, in its unfailing commitment to competition in all arenas of life but most spectacularly in her private sector. I have encountered fewer fiercer forces than the corporate and capitalist of this nation. It is a matter of course that in the life of the American business or company, it is forced to rediscover, revitalize, re-imagine, and remake; such are the consequences of robust competition and perpetual threat, and such is the self-made nature of the society in which the business finds itself. In such societies as this, innovation becomes intrinsic, benefiting the consumer. The great inventions for which this man is renowned; his steamboat, telegraph, steel plow, reaper, telephone, phonograph and assembly line, all offer the evidence of existence of the unprecedented and exceptional innovation that has delivered to him commensurate wealth.

Average Is Unacceptable

I find that the man here knows not the word average, or if he does, recognizes better than most that the notion of average is most fluid; he knows he requires the extra. The business of this land boasts that his service or product is the world's best; a synchronized reflection of his confidence and his disdain for the relative, and that he is most subject to competition. I note with deep interest and great applause that it is just as common in the workplace of this land today to witness innovation in its traditional—from the top down—hierarchical structure as it is to discover equivalent innovation from the bottom up; circumstances due in no small part to this man's transformation of the world through technological advances.

The American consumes with an ardency and avidity unlike any outsider; he is even likely to refer to a product by the leading provider of same. Consumption does not rest its head even momentarily here, with the businesses of this man attempting with great intensity to accommodate the every desire of the customer. It appears to me that there is no event sufficiently minor, any time inconvenient or any moment too insubstantial for this man they call an American to conduct business or consume. I am struck wherever I find myself in this expanse of land that this is true; from the produce stores of the Amish in Pennsylvania, to the six-year-old in Memphis performing tumble turns on Beale Street, to the lemonade stalls of the young ambitious girl in the neighborhood of central Illinois, these matters transcend geography, culture, or style. The consumerism which is infused in this man, to the point of being overstocked, I must add, demands entrepreneurship, and it is delivered with the dearest of relish. All over this nation at any one time, the visitor is liable to detect the unmistakable whirring of the business engine. Entrepreneurship and innovation is far and wide across this land, even in the unlikeliest of territories; religion, the example most striking.

The outsider finds much familiar in this land; an unsurprising and expectant revelation, considering the giant brands of this man have become the brands of the outsider. The man here, due to this exceptionalism, finds himself at home almost anywhere in the world, and when he finds himself confronted with unfamiliarity, he has the good judgment to immediately endow it with familiarity, such as the Green Zone of his military outpost. It is such readiness and conviction that are apt to outrage the men of many other nations but it is not so much that this man cares little for such opinion; it is that his passion of belief. The super business brands of the American provide his land with substantive support and soft power, a matter that again he seems to not completely appreciate. His drink of Coca-Cola is one of more than two hundred countries, and his restaurant of McDonalds with more than thirty thousand of its number worldwide show this; not to mention the cinema of this land, better known by its metonym, Hollywood, that receives in excess of half of its revenue from outside this nation I find myself in. As with his military, the man here celebrates his business accomplishments, glorifying them; the World of Coke and the CNN center both in the magnificent city of Atlanta can only delight an outsider, as they indent on him the world exceptionalism of the domestic business.

The successful entrepreneur of this land, I find, is often more likely to have a checkered past than not; this is, after all, a land of risk and measureless opportunity. It is, therefore, most common for the inordinately successful businessman to have been at one time a bankrupt, perhaps even more than this one occasion. But it would appear almost no fate consigns the businessman to failure in this country, no mistake or failing capable of finishing his ambitions. To the outsider, this is a most strange state of affairs; his is a much more unforgiving culture, with a pitiless emphasis on his reputation. The entrepreneur of this land, it is without doubt, benefits from redemption, optimism and a prevailing reluctance toward judgment; all positions directed by the Christian character of this man and his nation, with Biblical origin. It would appear once more that this exceptional man here diagnoses with success the reality that the genuine zeniths of achievements require the summits of failure to have been crossed. I find that the American not only tolerates a recovery entrepreneur; he is celebrated. More than this, I find that the greater the depths plunged; the higher the esteem for him. A mistake or failing is most easily redeemed in this land, and one can quickly return to public favor. In such a nation as this of risk-takers, it feels that such public response is most compatible and most reassuring to the human condition, spurring the man here to push the boundaries of his own exceptionalism in the wake of his seemingly unlimited chances.

The tertiary institution of this most venerable nation, in spite of its ever-accruing strongly leftist proclivity, is inestimable in pyramiding the exceptionalism of the man here. The existence of the university should serve as the first independent vehicle of the individual, and provide a campus with very limited traffic lights but many traffic circles; the former a symbol of restriction and control by authority, the latter a representation of freedom. The university of this land, I find, is exceptional in support of the individual and their entrepreneurial quest for success; nearly all the beasts of the information age were spawned in the computer labs of such educational providers across the land: Google, Microsoft, Facebook and Hewlett Packard. It is not uncommon for these projects and others of different scale to be encouraged, supported and prioritized by the administration and staff of the university here; in the case of the Google giant, it was the acclaimed institution of this man called Stanford University that committed even made a financial investment. While I do not say that the first-class university cannot be found in a great number of lands, indeed they can and do in large number but it is true, I must say, that those operating within the confines of the culture striving for mediocrity are by nature saddled with socialistic gravitation and pessimism, making an investment of belief in such projects a difficult proposition. The university in the foreign land has been known to even refuse to hold the published books of its alumni in their libraries; books that sit comfortably and happily in the shelves of the National Library of Congress in this great land; a tragic contrast to the American experience. This is not to say the tertiary institution is compulsory for success; it is here again the visitor can only amaze at this man's ability to come good; lest it be forgotten that four of the greatest companies of the world today were founded by four of this man's number failing in their college education, men of names Bill Gates, Mark Zuckerberg, Michael Dell, and Steve Jobs.

An Entrepreneurial Spirit

I discover the American cares little for his reputation, compared to his English-speaking cousin; he is, after all, an individual with his own dream, a matter immensely respected in this non-collectivist society. From birth, I cannot doubt that the American is more prone than the outsider to become an entrepreneur or exhibit entrepreneurial quality. This sets him up, fiercely individualistic, for another inevitable intersection with the collective, this time in the essential terrain of business; and again I am struck by the extraordinary outcome: the collision is resolved in favor of the collective at the benefit of the individual once more. It must be said that the great entrepreneur comprehends that he who serves best profits most and that he must offer service above himself; it is, I think, hardly a coincidence that these are the words of slogans reflective of the Rotarian spirit, a humanitarian service unsurprisingly born in this country. Service, in this land, I can report is heavily personalized, echoic of the predominantly individual emphasis of the culture. It is not uncommon, in the light of such service, for the man here to be easily convinced to make a purchase of greater value; the selling strategies of up-selling and cross-selling birthed by men of his exceptional number, with their unparalleled grasp on the psychology of the consumer, gluing service ethos and selling potential. Such ingenuity has influenced the sale of goods, and in its absence, I posit many businesses of the American and the outsider would not exist; the man of the outside world does increasingly embrace the service ethos first set by that of the man here.

The general energy and optimism of this man spills into the workplace; carefully harnessed by employers I find to be sage, men who lead all lands in the business concept of motivation for employees, pivotal in their retention and loyalty. The American employee, whether a white, blue or green colored worker, impresses as far more greatly personally invested in the company for which he works, than the outsider. I note him speaking of his place of employment often with great reverence; like he or the outsider might speak of their favorite sporting team. The encouragement to speak and act freely means the man of this nation is unreserved and passionate, and unashamed to advertise his place of employment. It is also true, I have no choice in saying, that he is more disposed to respect his superiors within the workplace than his outsider counterpart may be; this is a nation that values the successful, untainted by the socialist paint that insists no one individual is any more successful than any other. It is of course foreseeable that the praise of an employer in such context is much more greatly powerful, engendering the potentially more harmonious relationship. The man here that is an employee of the business or company defining of the small community in which he resides is most allegiant. I find such man to care deeply for his place of employment as he integrates his community with his work; he desires little more than a reputation as industrious, steadfast in his commitment and proficient in his work; the outside employer left to dream for just one employee of such mindset.

The business here mirrors the American; both possessing an indissoluble, and spoken, desire to be the best. While the outsider frowns at or smites self-promotion, a practice considered ill-mannered in a culture of socialist-driven mediocrity, the American largely embraces it and is its greatest practitioner. These matters are manifest; in the society of which man is reliant on government and anchored by its largesse, the promotion of oneself is unnecessary and therefore viewed with derision; in the truly free society in which government is limited and the individual has only himself, his family and church on which to rely, such promotion is not only beneficial but necessary for survival. So it is here, in this land.

Performance reigns supreme in the workplace of this man; family background, education and status are here entirely immaterial to the employer, as they may not be in other societies. The culture of performance within the businesses of this land is most famed and require little amplification; it is the key to the lock of exceptionalism and leadership. I find that the mediocre employee here has no place in the fierce, highly charged and unforgiving landscape of the corporate or business in this land. Similarly, the man here boldly declares publicly his aspiration; promotion in this country is not left to chance, I discover; here an employee does not wait patiently for the employer to privately signal approval, as he is prone to do in other cultures, as any other action is deemed to be of poor form. In this land that is America, it must be stated that the employer encourages his employee to flaunt entrepreneurial flair, compete and exceed his potential, and he is, from what I have seen, liable to reward it accordingly. It is in this vein, I observe the mentality of the waiter or waitress across this land to be unlike those to which the visitor would be accustomed in his homeland; the American filling this role is always seeking to deliver the additional, the extra. Even as I travel through the rural of this country, I find even the itinerant worker of the farmlands and other vocations are impregnated with similar disposition.

I have little doubt that the franchise is the greatest export of this man and his unabashed capitalistic nature; it has enabled men of all nations to own and run a business, simultaneously spreading to virtually all corners of the world the most cherished values of freedom, liberty, individualism, and bringing to fruition the opportunity for the pursuit of happiness. The home of the franchise is, of course, this land; only this nation could have developed a concept so embodying of the values it espouses. It is here its introduction and implementation were first overseen; a fact seldom acknowledged by the men quick to decry the capitalism of this land. It is clear that the dreams of many men for a life beyond their ancestors have been culminated through a business innovation, with its genesis in this country.

It has been often said of the man here by those inside and outside with little affection for his land that he is incapable of fostering positive relations in the world, beyond the borders of his land. I find no evidence of these matters; the man here may well be untraveled but he is most capable of this; were he not, one would expect him and the business for which he works, employing of men and women from across many diverse lands and ensuring of their loyalty and motivation, to be incapable of such employment and retention, and such an assertion can only be characterized as absurd.

This nation, I find, is advantaged immeasurably by the thrift of its people; the old Protestant work ethic most alive, his capitalism in no small part benefited by the economic dynamism, a consequence of the Protestant reformation.

The American connects and collaborates like no other; it is both thrilling and mesmerizing to observe the man of the city here in his daily routine. His pace is frenzied, his actions immediate with no second wasted; he is the ultimate multitasker. This is a man with a proactive nose, permanently seeking the fresh scent of the new connection or opportunity, with his business card and personal technology his only essentials. On the other hand, I find the semi-rural American operates with similar effect and organization but with slower pace, but retaining a hyper-connectivity. The man here is a born networker; I can think of no other industrialized country where business networking is as conspicuous as it is in this land.

His networking capacity is ideal for the intersection of globalization and information technology; such technology witness to new mediums and messages. I find the American thoroughly addicted to his technology; he has selflessly and unwittingly imparted his technological innovation and commitment to the outside world. But these matters have threatened the man here; his acts, again motivated by his values and convictions for all individuals, have enhanced enormously mankind but also business everywhere; to the point, where men of all nations enjoys an almost level playing field with the business of this land. That is to say, the man of this nation has ensured that the remote country town of Western Australia is today the neighbor and business partner of the fishing village of India. There is not a place, I feel as I engage in life here, in this man's life which, through innovative communications technology, has not enhanced his capitalist nature; even the church is online, the worship virtual. The twin mattresses of globalization and information technology and their common materials mean the American sleeps uniquely, but not without challenge. In his daily life, the American here operates with the ease expected of the man that has built the world of all men. But I cannot help but note, with cautionary tone, that these are also the circumstances of complacency; an enemy of even greater magnitude than the old Soviet bear.

I find the businesses of this country are not without their weakness, but it would appear that the claims of providence by this man may be true; even its internal weaknesses appear to strengthen the world. The society of this man is the most litigious in the world; he is quicker than any I have known to meet with the man of the law. This most unsavory, in my view, reality has ensured the most rigorous occupational health and safety standards, operational programs and staff training are applied here in this country, and then in the workplaces of the many other lands. It is unclear to me whether these matters will remain without the exercise of vigilance in the future; I note the steady increase in governmental presence in the workplace of this of this land, especially in the industries of food and the automobile.

The predisposition of the American for risk is not always rewarded; but dislocation appears only possible in temporary form in this land with its boomerang spirit, with the man here always recovering, and upon his return, capable only of increasing his exceptionalism, it seems. There does appear to be in this land consistency in this ability as I cast my eye over its history over any number of events, ranging from financial crises to war. The American boomerang has been ever active, from early defeats by Britain in the War of Independence, to the days following Pearl Harbor, to the loss of the Philippines to the events of its most horrific terrorist attack a decade previous.

Chapter 7
CHARACTER

Any visiting outsider emerges himself in America with the quickest of pace, thoroughly ensconcing himself in the daily life of the American. He swiftly deduces that the strength of this land lies in her celebration of individuality; this man appears to believe in it almost in every sense of the word. I find that this celebration accounts for the incomparable and distinctive diversity of the American, and the extremities that exist; the latter, of course, hastily pounced on by this man's enemies as evidence of his hypocrisy. The palpability of this diversity, influenced by any number of variables, including at least geography and demography, prompts many to hold the position of the American historian and definer of modern liberalism in this country, Henry Steele Commager:

> Every effort to confine Americanism to a single pattern, to constrain it to a single formula, is disloyalty to everything that is valid in Americanism.

It is entirely true that the American is most difficult to diagnose, and that the great freedom of this man imbues him with one of the most powerful senses of free will. But

Exceptional America

each nation has both soul and narrative, and this man, I can only conclude, has perhaps the grandest of each. This is not the only such determination that may be made; adopting the relativist perspective dismisses any qualitative effort to understand cultural phenomena which reflect the knowledge and system of meanings intrinsic to the life of a cultural group. It must be said for the purposes of logic and in the tenor of this man's freedom: to juice cultural information and proceed to ascribe certain characteristics to the said culture or the character of the people within it, after careful analysis and observation is not only legitimate, but required of participation in free social discourse. Character belongs not just to the individual but to the country, I would advance.

There does exist an American who best represents, in sum, this nation. He is, for example, the American who believes that God is the root cause of his blessings and opportunities, as opposed to the outsider with his feeble glances to his government to offer him mere shadows of opportunities. I must disagree with Commager; for I believe that if Americanism is everything, then it is nothing. His assertion belies the bed of values that this man clings to obstinately, and at great price. A string of misconceptions, it is revealed to me in striking color as I roam about, exist about the man of this land in the minds of the outsider also. Humanity will, it is a matter of course, always produce the sin of hypocrisy but exceptions, such as those that the forces against this man covet, do not disprove the general rule. I must also comment that this nation is not without the ills plaguing the men of other nations at this time, in fact, I find evidence of disturbing regularity that many such ailments begin within the borders of this nation, but have failed to penetrate the national culture or demography.

Nick Adams

The prolonged visit here reveals to me, with great force and notable repetition, strains of thought and waves of values held aggressively; gratitude, optimism, pride and spirituality rating highly among them. The character of the American is an intricately sewn quilt, patchwork in many ways. His faith which he wears on his sleeve moulds him; his attitude guided by his Constitution, a grandly unique document which I can simply not cease to be impressed with; this is the one document of its kind, I can think of, which is not a stipulation of the power of the government bur an outline of the citizen's rights.

But most outstanding in this man, despite all his mercantilism, is his faithful appreciation of the simple matters of life; matters of permanent traditional presence and of most meaning. He casts here only sullen looks at those that have or seek the sullying of tradition. I am reminded of the musings of philosopher and transcendentalist, Henry David Thoreau in his book, Walden, a reflection upon simple living in natural surroundings, as I meander the aisles of this man's inconceivably enormous shopping centers observing him:

> The mass of men lead lives of quiet desperation, and most men, even in this comparatively free country, through mere ignore and mistake, are so occupied with the factitious cares and superfluously coarse labours of this life that its finer fruits cannot be plucked by them.

Priorities

The priorities of life in a country the scale of this man's vary, as they do even within the course of the individual life. But deep in the areas of the real America, the visiting outsider enters cities, towns, and suburbs and notes that the priorities within these populations have undergone scant change, and cannot escape the conclusion that upon his return in fifty years, little will have altered. The visitor to these parts is a curious learner, captivated. To the outsider, likely acquainted with the steady erosion of tradition and the sad replacement of selfless community service with self-interest, he amazes in the homecoming tradition to welcome back alumni or former residents on a sunny Friday afternoon that that see residential streets lined with people sitting on their lawn; he gasps at the 1950s images of his own nation of the street parade full of young children on tricycles affixed with American flags; he shocks at the devotion to church organization; he marvels at the traditional gender roles of community organization, with men gathering ironically, as a collective, and the women, of this land, too. The comforts of tasty comfort food and drink are prized here; the American may work harder than the outsider but whatever time he has, he enjoys deeply. This land, I must say, reminds me of the mental images of natural, normal and healthy life; one formerly of an automatic reality across the lands of the West. If the outsider is over the vintage of fifty, nostalgia would be his most probable response. And on the matter of nostalgia: I see no man here without it, an unsurprising state given his emotional intensity. He, of this land, is the type liable to declare that nostalgia is not what it used to be.

Nick Adams

While it is unfortunately true the many elites of the outside world and the few that reside in pockets of this nation have drowned their minds with the waves of the swelling sea of secularism, the man here understands the civic consequences of his religion; he recognizes its role in fostering good citizenship. The foreigner cannot help but be impressed by the level of activity of the American in civic life, a shining trait beamed across this land with full force. The areas of life and character in the American home are not extinguished by the tall lining trees of the government driveway; they remain light-filled. The outsider feels in his own nation he breathes but he does not exist; his insides doleful, his energy quashed, his creativity squelched, his ambition funereal. Such, and it should be said with great sadness, is the nature of the country whose cultural nose immediately guides it to the addictive smells of the insatiable government, whatever its predicament. In this grand nation, the same outsider is exhilarated and emancipated, swept away by the winds of opportunity and limitlessness; liberty opened with the relish of the child brandishing a can of pop, awaiting animatedly its exciting and refreshing opening click, and accompanying gush of air and life. Titillating and arresting, this release of compression allows access to the liquid of true liberty; an intoxicating fluid that nourishes the soul, remitting his power to distinguish himself and returning his ability to pierce through and achieve with his talent.

A Simple Family Life

The American appears contented with his simple life; not coveting that which belongs to others. I believe it to be true, certainly of my experiences that the man here,

Exceptional America

although living in the most capitalistic of cultures, is most capable of enjoying his life with little money; he finds great joy in his wife and children. He shows little interest if another man has more wealth than he; this changes only in the event that the man, as a result of such wealth, has power over him. The act of coveting, there is no doubt, colors the character, washes over the wills and motivates to malice. It would appear from my journeys that the traditions and the attitudes engendered by such life that this man clings to with the whitest of knuckles, guards him broadly against the approaches that wilt the personality and constrain the heart. To observe the American family is at once endearing and inspirational; it is, at least on the surface, the most idealized familial image. I cannot help but feel, from the organized party of children at the local video arcade to the family lunch after this man's Sunday church service to the local Little League baseball game to the annual professional photographs I find to sit in great number on the walls and showcases of his home, that the family is at its most natural and greatest in this nation. This man here is the most child-oriented of men; his lifestyle shaped around his children.

The emphasis on the child in this polity bears intensity unmatched in any The emphasis on the child in this polity bears intensity unmatched in any parallel society; one need only look at the party industry spawned in this country or modern-day Disney to understand. It is at the age of eighteen, I discover, that the American almost invariably begins his journey of independence; a baby eagle pushed out of his nest by his mother, reluctantly but for his own good. The adult eagle wants to see if her child can fly; she understands that life and flight are in the struggle; without struggle, there can be no growth. As I journey through the hills of this place, I wonder if this is a remnant of the great frontier age of this nation when boy became man by leaving civilization blazing a trail toward these very hills. The nations of the outsider nest their children for much greater time, often refusing to allow their young to grow; there is in them a culture wishing for man to extend his adolescence for as much as he can that I find to be conspicuously absent here. The irony of this parallel to the desires of the self-appointed intellectual guardians of same society is striking with their objective to turn the adult into the infant. Here, this is absent, and yet again I am once more struck at this man's ability to coalesce his family orientation with reality, a utilitarian streak seemed reserved for such matters of life.

It is perhaps this shorter time span that imposes on the American a far deeper emphasis on his children; he effectively has only eighteen years to shape his child before his child's presence becomes part-time. The man here always finds a reason or season to celebrate with the family and friends of his community; the graduation, Father's Day, Memorial Day and Mother's Day major events in the American calendar; I cannot imagine, nor does it appear, there to be a time this man does not consider worthy of festivity.

The Bonds of Friendship

The religious observance of the citizens of this nation, the outsider finds, not only cements the American's status as a conscientious citizen, but sews his community with its common thread. Through it, he is mobilized or consoled, uplifted or redeemed. The social networks of this land, I can report, are more than often infused with religious connection, entrenching friendship and identity. Among these networks of this man, friendship and relationship are the most passionate and enduring of affairs. Such is the significance and power of these relationships that the outsider often feels he encounters a family more than a community, and a family home more than a town or major centre. Community, faith and family are seen rightly by this man as that which he owes his first duty; an attitude any individual wishing to function with liberty must fiercely abide as it curtails the authority and guillotines the ambition of the state. The man here is further bound by the superglue of his Constitution; a document that provides the powerful adhesive of local decisions, spurring active citizenry and civic pride, binding a community together. These circumstances, I must say are most laudable when considered in context; they exist in a time where the rise of technology presides over the diminishment of the traditional community; that it is the same man responsible for that technology is not an irony to be lost. What may well have begun with the personalized Sony Walkman of 1980, the dissolution of the local community has only been buttressed by continued innovation. Yet the exceptional American shows not the barest of signs that his technology has interfered with the frequency of his interaction with his local community; to the contrary, I find great evidence that this man has managed to use the advances of technology to enhance communal presence and morale, as a tool of organization, mobilization and communication.

On Leadership

The American is a zealous guardian of social orthodoxies. His penchant for the order of nature means he is prepared to allow one to lead, where the outsider, and particularly the European, does not. To refuse to follow is a most praiseworthy trait when its motivation is steeped in individualism; when founded in the socialistic mire suggesting no one person or opinion should be considered extraordinary, it is a most disagreeable and detrimental characteristic. If the choice is not to follow, then leadership is its only viable alternative; the problem for the outsider is that his culture and therefore character makes him unlikely to be disposed to leadership. The absence of leadership is no virtue. The chronological consequence of which is a nation of neither leaders nor followers. The man here permits natural order and instinctively follows if impressed; equally impelled by merit and primal reason. He subconsciously sees the broad shoulders of a man as a symbol of destiny; a sign of God's will for him to lead. The American is a man urged more by the primal than any other; the primacy of the primal clear, the American throws his support and organization behind the aspiring leader that has impressed with a force most uncommon. Nature is no force for the outsider, long ago discarded by him; a man acclimatized to the tinkering of nature for political or cultural advantage, always looking for man-made solution. In much the same way, the soul of the man of this land innately magnetizes and protects the nature of man, understanding the real imperilment posed by the overly ambitious government. In his thinking, the American allows his land to be the greatest representation of nature; a requirement for the exceptional man, clearly understanding the tampering hand of the man is most unnatural. His great strength is that he preserves the nature and spirit of man's individual character.

Flexible and Gracious

While a man of enormous comfort and the engineer of such a world, the American, I find, falls not easily to complacency; always prepared and exuding flexibility. His litheness is noticeably absent in matters of tradition where he escapes the gravitational pull, but aggressively apparent in matters of self-improvement when the national or community interest is at stake, exhorted to greater effort, spurning new bursts of creativity from within. He is not a man likely to collapse into hysterical laughter but certainly one that enjoys humor. He is a man comfortable and cherishing of physical space in all manner; the visitor encroaches any two-foot boundary at his peril. Depending where the visitor finds himself, the American will speak with a different accent and variable syntax. But wherever he is, he speaks with a throaty voice, lending depth and authority; his purpose of language more often one of persuasion, with accompanying suitable cadence, than what the outsider is accustomed. A casual man, he reverts to the first name quickly, in the absence of exceptional circumstance. While it may vary somewhat on region, I find him to be a most polite man. I seldom encounter an established man here unhappy with his place of residence; in fact he is likely to say he would not live elsewhere.

The American is a most thankful man, glad to be alive; a condition helped in no small way by his religiosity. It is, of course, the tendency of man to be most appreciative within the raised stakes of survival; a man of the artificial world buffered by government and others cannot grasp the realities of the world, and is correspondingly powerless in understanding them. Gratitude is the guard against the engines of envy and greed; the temperance of this man's desire for upward mobility. He lives and gives with an open hand and heart, seemingly understanding that a tied hand accompanies a tied heart. He adheres to the noting of the ancient writer of the Book of Proverbs, unsurprisingly, three thousand years ago: Do not withhold good from those who deserve it when it is in your power to act.

The American, the visitor discovers, is a robust and proficient man, considering the continuing life of the mind in non-intellectual pursuits, meaningful work, deep relationships and the pursuit of the virtues of gratitude, generosity and foundational to the authentically contented life; underpinnings he is able to take responsibility for, not captive to externals. Despite his individualism, he appears to most stalwartly that self-absorption is the enemy of self-contentment. This is a man who enters tepid waters without glee; he wades out into the stream of success with speed, often waist deep, filled with energy and unyielding determination. He is the type of man, I find, to feel that if where there is a will, he feels there is a way; this is compared to the more likely completion of the phrase by other men: where there is a will, I want to be in it.

He is always prepared to serve his country to assist in overcoming a national challenge or problem, regardless of his own abilities. While an emotional man, he is almost always focused on the practical; in line with de Tocqueville's assessment centuries ago:

> A thousand special causes have singularly concurred to fix the mind of the American upon purely practical objects. His passions, his wants, his education, and everything about him seem to unite in drawing the native of the United States earthward.

American Pride

The American is often demonized for his pride and no dispute can exist: this man is a prideful individual. He is often painted by the world elite as a man buoyant and smoothly gliding on the winds of hubris—the same that can send men of power to dizzying heights. But I cannot find, as I rove his countless counties, any evidence to support this. Confidence threatens the insecure man, and is not without its dangers. But the American has a valid reason for his pride; muck akin to the fan excited for his championship-winning football team, the man of this land knows he has achieved true success, for which pride is justified. He is not interested in trumpeting about false claims to greatness; rather, the American realizes that his cultural and individual achievements are worthy of praise; a reality in which he revels and glories. This reality of recognition of true achievement propels him forward; a matter deserving of motivation for the men of other lands and not a denigration of the American. He has reason to be proud and the outsider opportunity to be proud, as well. The virtue of humility is not modesty; to be humble is not to deny one's own talents or gifts but to influence others and exercise those talents and gifts for the good of others, and not for praise, adulation or internal reward.

The inescapable optimism of this land and its people, primarily borne of its great faith, aided by its geographical expansiveness and ceaseless opportunity for new beginning, and exemplified by its enormous open freeways, extends his arm direct to the heart of the visitor. Enthusiasm, the word of which the Greek origins comprise the two words "en" and "theos," or "in God," fittingly is deep in the American. The man here is unwilling to settle, knowing the cessation of his search or pursuit of his dream will condemn him to drudgery; a fate the American refuses to accede, a craver of intrinsic reward. He seizes opportunity; demands them. I find him to be brimming with the self-assured bonhomie expected of a man of his nature and strength. He seeks from his profession, it would seem, much the same outcomes of the Christian faith: renewal, enrichment and reinvigoration. He is a transient man that uproots himself regularly, more so than that of any other man of any other nation. He is likely to have moved within the last decade at least twice; often well beyond the borders of his county or state. His transience is not a matter of instability; merely these actions reflect the irresistible lust for the fresh adventure of this man, his aversion to risk and his perpetual pursuit of the American dream. It seems to the foreign observer that seldom there is a minute in the life of the American that his subconscious is not dedicated to the pursuit of his Declaration of Independence right to pursue happiness. Christianity, when practiced with God's intentions, carries enormous happiness, comfort, security and satisfaction; religion and life satisfaction wedded in the church. It therefore of logical progression, and occasioning only scarce surprise to the outsider, that the American is a man dedicated to or seeking of religion.

The man of this land, I perceive to understand the simple rules of the happy life; he recognizes that low expectations trap the holder in mediocrity. I find him to know than any other man that the wrong thinking pattern imprisons in defeat, understanding that the bitter root can only produce the bitter fruit. He realizes that words affect his children's future and I see great substantiation all over this land that he therefore encourages, inspires and motivates through loving words. These matters often have the men of foreign lands accusing the American of syrupy words; it is truthful that acerbic pithiness is most uncommon when the man here converses in his unique and pungent expression, in the tongue of optimism. If he is guilty of such offence, it must be said he is a most upstanding delinquent. The ma here is the most loquacious and gregarious of all men, a further paradox. Within this optimism lies a faithful acceptance; the American is not a man of belief in the law of nature like his outside cousin, rejecting karma and instead accepting that at times bad people prosper while good people suffer, most likely a carry-over of the Christian faith. The American seems to have an answer to every problem; the outsider a problem for every answer. He has, I find, as his answer always mankind or the individual where the outsider, sees societal reinvention through government or education. Where the American harbors optimism in his fellow man, the non-American is directed by his ruling elites to moor himself in misanthropy; to be frustrated and fretful about the poisonous influence of mankind, considering the nature of man to be the most substantial roadblock to the society of perfection.

He is a man with an appreciation that success must first be conceived in heart and mind before it materializes; the same way his SEAL's belief in accomplishing his mission transcends all environmental or physical obstacles that threaten failure. I find that the man here rarely makes the debilitating error of shifting from the dreaming program to the maintenance program. The visitor finds that while the American is most partial to his historic past, he is adoring of the modern and the future; an observation first made by de Tocqueville just a few decades after the founding of this nation when he noticed "a sort of distaste for what is ancient."

Nick Adams

As a man of deep insight, but not always stability, the American has almost always displayed the supreme virtue of being unafraid to act. The hardwiring of this man here provides him with the steely ability to see over the horizon while the outsider struggles with poor vision. He covets leadership; this land educates for leadership like no other. The American knows his product is unique and continues to produce it; the product is individually trained in liberty and motivated by freedom which proceeds to spread American values and spirit, both home and abroad. The foreigner is continually astounded at the depth of his liberty; he understands there is little reason to celebrate the existence of the democratic election if the government is too powerful. The man here asks: what good brings my ability to choose the guardian if my guardian is to operate in the context of an overly powerful and centralized government? He asks these questions of liberty, for deep in his granite soul, he feels a slight shiver every time he sees the Old Glory. Individualism, true assimilation and self-improvement are the values of the true American man. He fiercely eschews the radical egalitarian policies that menace exceptionality and democracy; a philosophy that is contrary to the state of man and his Creator's plan for him and serves as a disincentive to achievement. A man without conviction finds tolerance natural; it is, therefore, understandable that the American is the most intolerant of men. He is in remarkably in touch with humanity; while he may travel little, the variety of his people, make him most in tune.

The outsider exposed to the geographical diversity of this land, dependent on the variables of personality and experience, finds true exceptionalism in each of the states of what is known as America. But it is most challenging to dispute the presence of the mammoth state that sits in the south-west of the continental landmass in any discussion of American exceptionalism; a state of mind and area, almost a nation. The land of Texas is enough to excite any man's lust; a place that lingers with the visitor. The Texan is the most American of the Americans; a fearsome man irrespective of physical size, he walks with unmistakable moxie and possesses an unfailing courtesy punctuated only in the event of provocation in which his already almost indecipherable drawl becomes impossibly more pronounced. He requires no words to make his displeasure clear; one needs only cast a cursory glance in his eyes. The Texan is a man of tradition, family, masculinity, hospitality, generosity, self-reliance, patriotism and God; a fortress of common sense, directness and traditional values. It would appear that the stories of the Texan are all true; there is almost nothing he cannot do. Even if outnumbered and outgunned, the visitor feels the Texan is never out of the fight. In her fifteen major rivers, not one is a deep river of negativity. The Texan surrounds himself in faith, with even a monument of the Ten Commandments on the grounds of his State Capitol, and he understands that he cannot soar with the eagles if he pecks with the chickens. His state is a frontier, a lamp unto the feet of the American, and a light unto his path; if the American were ever to require guidance, the Texan, I feel, should be his first contact. It is hard for the outsider to imagine that such a society as the Texan's exists; truly the finest of human society. The inspiring words of the heroic Navy SEAL and model of strength and virtue hailing from East Texas, Marcus Luttrell, surprise the visitor little and are instructive for the embattled American:

> . . . most of all, I am an American. And when the bell sounds, I will come out fighting for my

> country and for my teammates. If necessary, to the death.
>
> And that's not just because the SEALs have trained me to do so; it's because I'm willing to do so. I'm a patriot, and I fight with the Lone Star of Texas on my right arm and another Texas flag over my heart. For me, defeat is unthinkable.

The presence of the South Carolinian in the southeast of this nation is another imbuing the finest of exceptionalism. Utterly individualistic, the South Carolinian lives in a society defined by the power of the state, not federal. He, second only to the Texan, values the individual and the individual state above all else, including the federal government. It was the state of South Carolina to first declare war on the federal government in 1861, waiting just four days after the election of Lincoln to begin the process; the same fiery conviction that the state should run the state, rather than the federal government, has not changed in the last century and a half. The South Carolinian remains as the bearer of only one of two states in the federal union to sponsor its own military academy; a relic of the statist fervor felt before the outbreak of the American Civil War, but remaining today, a powerful symbol of state superiority over federal jurisdiction. He is a man defined by tradition, but molded by modernity; a man who affirms his past, but more importantly, affirms his future. The people of South Carolina are hardly dinosaurs mired in racist, bigoted past but revolutionaries emboldened by the widespread opportunities of a new era. Both he and the Texan have a life that is authentically theirs.

Such observations of the American character do not suggest that the American is better than the outsider by birth; this is simply untrue, for both are members of humanity and given life by God. It can be said that the man here, whether by nature or nurture, is raised with an expectation of opportunity and a conviction in self-worth that the outsider may never achieve or attain, owing his often socialistic and equivocating upbringing. It remains a matter of uncertainty if the outsider will achieve the greatness of his American cousin. Discomfort always accompanies the perception of second-place but this grand land, it must be said, has not become the winner by cheating or falsifying her achievements. I feel an identical level of greatness is within the grasp of the outsider, if he has the courage to shun statism and embrace and celebrate the fruit of the individual spirit that American has juiced since his founding. The celebration of this man of his legitimate achievements need not be exclusive; the outsider need only reject its statist present and past in favor of an American-style acceptance of the individual to celebrate commensurately the feast of plenty that this land and her people currently enjoy.

God in Culture

The visitor is stirred deeply at the American sporting event of any magnitude; it resembles more an august spectacle or celebration than a mere physical clash. This is an occasion the man here seizes to parade proudly each of the streamers of sentiment and exceptionalism: patriotism, military, Christianity, individualism, family, competition and size. Match or game; each is preceded with pyrotechnic prowess, and devotion and tribute to the military, national anthem and prayer, the interesting interplay uniting to electrify any in the vicinity. It is in this presence of the modern day gymnasia that the breath of the visitor vanishes, and he truly grasps in this one moment the philosophy, history, geography, sociology and law of the American.

It would appear to me that even the non-religious men and women of this nation welcome the influence of God, if even only in the abstract. Even the secular American speaks often unwittingly the vocabulary of faith, and its succeeding optimism, testimony to the penetrating power of the civil religion that has taken permanent residency in this national culture. Underpinning his utterances are his actions. The three columns of optimism, faith and individuality provide the high-pitched roof of abundance, size and continual increase. The American appears to follow more closely than any other man known to me the words of Genesis 1:28 (NIV):

> *God blessed them, saying: Be fruitful and multiply, and fill the earth, and subdue it; and rule over the fish of the sea and over the birds of the sky and over every living thing that moves on the earth.*

The visitor here feels small; I can do little but marvel at the staggering physical size of everything in this land. Size is to the American what seed is to the sower, and bread to the eater; it is not jumbled and intermittent but constant and commanding. From the sunlight of early dawn to the darkness of night, the almost imperious physical size of his streets, automobiles, buildings, meals, shopping stores and choices whips the visitor to almost frenzied enthusiasm. He knows instinctively even in the face of a hitherto life of limited travel that no other such land could have exiled the small or average with the brutality of the American. The visitor quickly connects the correlation of size to cultural attitude; the physical surroundings of his own land positively dwarfed by that of the American. It is true that the landmass of the American is more likely greater than the outsider and that his was a planned nation but this factual matter is simplistic in the appraisal of this man's culture and dedication to size. The symbol of luxury and blessing, it appears the core belief shared by the man here that he live his life in the plenty, and be fruitful. Meaningfully, it is tied to his politics. While the ruling elites of the international world posit, with the dutiful obedience of the outsider, the need to pare down the life of the human for environmental grounds, this man, largely, and certainly to greater degree than any other, rightfully in my view, ignores these secular interventions. The men of other lands, it must be said however unpopular, have been conditioned to feel a tangible morality if he personally sacrifices for the "overall good of the planet" while his ruling elite rub their hands in glee in the socialistic corridors of government buildings at the achievement of the redistribution of the wealth through novel taxation, removing competitive advantage and destroying the public sector. The onslaught of these matters has encouraged the use of the smaller vehicle and residence; the natural progression of which will be the shrinking of the family. The American, while wishing to bequeath a healthy environment to his children, I find shudders at the approach of the elite that suggests that man alone is responsible for nature; that God is absent.

The man here, as I have asserted appears most suspicious of men claiming to be more intelligent; a form of seemingly paradoxical egalitarianism on the part of this man most interesting. The source of the attitude of these men of intellect who consider their fellow man inferior and in need of supervision, regulation, and guidance derives of their belief they have been conditioned to think for themselves; an aptitude beyond reach of the ordinary man of tradition and prejudice inherited. But I, having assessed these matters must say that the difference of these men to the American, and indeed the ordinary men of every nation, lies not with education but indoctrination. The elite whether he hails from this land or any other has, as a result of his education an almost unanimous and uniform position on every matter of culture, society or political policy; a consensus that renders the basis of his alleged superiority of independent thought entirely erroneous. These are men of programming and indoctrination, not education and independent thought; a conclusion the so-called common man can most easily draw. Common sense is the currency of this man, for it is printed on Main Street.

The Battle and Ballet of the Sexes

The American loves his personal land; his house is his castle and refuge. Land and liberty are most interwoven in the minds of this man, a remaining mindset of his early history; a continuation of his reaction to the British government attempting to confine further settlement. Here he sings the tune of his greatest, George Washington, in his view of land and property. The outsider does note with concern the growing regulation in the building of the American family home, as well as all the appliances found within them; reminiscent of his own lands. Four decades of the Cold War, and increasing international turbulence has it not uncommon for the man here to be equipped, both mentally and physically for international invasion or domestic attack. The uninvited man on the property of the American is brave; such is the passion and attachment of this ma to his land, again a clear product of masculine mentality. Again it is here that he either by coincidence or design, I cannot be sure, exhibits his exceptionality of understanding; he knows that his property is the safe of his liberty; once it is opened and conquered, the doors to each other area of his life are ripe harvest for the ambitions of the elites and political class.

If I had only one word with which to describe the man here, I would use bold. It is perhaps the most underrated compliment man can pay. It is in these contexts then that perhaps the pick-up truck of the American is his most apt symbol. A prized and most common possession of this man; it is, I offer, the ultimate personal construct of the American: an embodiment of his individualism, strength, protection and size. Its versatility enables him the convenient conduct of both business and charity work. A prideful vehicle, it encapsulates the masculinity of the American but not at the exclusion of the female; I cannot help but note the popularity of the vehicle with the American female. There is a little of the cowboy spirit in each American, male or female, and his or her shepherd is the Lord and much of the sheep station in the outsider, his shepherd the government.

The character of the man here must be understood in the circumstances; it is the character of a self-made man in the self-made society. The American is often considered by men of the outside lands to be rudimentary and unsophisticated; while this would still be incorrect, it is to be expected that he of this land carry the coarseness associated with such construction. This, I would say, includes the national character of this nation.

The American male exudes masculinity; the female radiating equivalent femininity. The man here cherishes his man-cave, that space of reverential silence in the family home, dedicated to male pursuits and interests. To the visiting outsider, familiar with the destructive graying of gender roles in his own and neighboring nations, such distinction and preservation of nature and tradition is most refreshing. Few of the number of the American male are effete or pampered. In the outsider Western nations, the feminization of society has weakened the traditional male to the point where he feels uncomfortable; rotated toward behavior anathematic to his instinct. The prescience of towering de Tocqueville critiqued the objectives of feminism long before its destructive second wave, and noted the American exceptionalism:

> There are people in Europe who, confounding together the different characteristics of the sexes, would make man and woman into beings not only equal but alike. They could give to both the same functions, impose on both the same duties, and grant to both the same rights; they would mix them in all things—their occupations, their pleasures, their business. It may readily be conceived that by thus attempting to make one sex equal to the other, both are degraded, and from so preposterous a medley of the works of nature nothing could ever result but weak men and disorderly women.

These matters and portrayal of gender are of limited revelation; they are entirely consistent with the famous characters of the literature and film of the American. Unlike the cultures of the European lands, the theme of romantic love barely exists; the classic masculine epic defined by his love for nature more than the female; the latter likely a target to rescue or the direction for a hat-tip. The masculine temperament in these narratives is diverse, but never is it explored in the context of sexual love; the man painted with the same colors of chastity used in the European's depiction of the female in his literature.

But the one departure of the fictional epics in reality is the American female in the American society; a true sight to behold. The American lady is a most powerful being; most exceptional in her dedication to family and organization in the important matters of church, community, charity and politics. Driven more by her values than perhaps some of her outsider counterparts, she is the rock of her family, and in times of crisis, her community and nation. She is the keeper of the family calendar. In the veins of each female here, I sense, courses the blood of the famous cultural icon, Rosie the Riveter. The American female is most certainly equal to the American man as the outsider female is to her male equivalent; she simply embraces with happiness her differences. The woman of this nation has, rightfully, greater prospects than her sisters of Europe; sectors of much industry virtual gynocracies. I find her to be brilliantly resourceful; the most American of traits.

The scope and number of this land, of course, mean that character will enjoy and suffer steep variance. The American is a man of great extremes, it must be said, and this is visible over his land, in every way. He can be a man of blindingly intense morals but as the outsider swivels his neck glancing at the well-dressed congregation of the Sunday morning, he knows the disparity of the public image of familial sanctity and the reality of the family discord, often savage. It cannot be denied that the American's contradictions can be most stark; a fact that the critical outsider is swift to remind of. In fact, often it feels so many contradictions exist, I cannot help but wonder how it is that the head of this man does not burst. Paradoxical it most surely is, that this man so revering of his leaders holds a record of four successful Presidential assassinations; that this nation of such robust Christianity has become the center of pornography, abortion and serial killers, and that this great ally of Israel and values-driven land backed away from truly moral action in the Suez Crisis of 1956. But these exceptions do not disprove the general rule. Paradox rises largest in the fertile soil of freedom. The level of pornographic access in Saudi Arabia, after all, would doubtlessly be far less than this nation but this is hardly an indication of superiority; merely an attestation to their lack of freedom. It must be remembered that freedom does not equal doing the right thing; it means having the chance to do the right thing. While the paradoxes of this nation are indeed ugly; it is not freedom that must be curtailed for this would destroy this wondrous land I find myself in love with. The American believes as much in the responsibility to do the right thing as he does in freedom. He is far from perfect, I recognize straying through his biggest cities, but he and his nation must remain the greatest example of human civilization, and the model for each nation to aspire, I feel. This conservative American that is to be found here is the primary manufacturer of exceptionalism and the warden of greatness; under him, his character and that of his nation is of immeasurable and unarguable greatness.

Chapter 8
CONSTITUTIONALLY LIMITED GOVERNMENT

The American has, it must be noted, a most keen interest and appreciation in his democratic beginnings. It was the Frenchman de Tocqueville that made the first outsider observation of the remarkability and exceptionalism of this man's ability to come together to meet a common objective. This grand thinker opined further that this capacity and appetite bred an active political and civil society, effectively safeguarding selfless patriotism through these acts of unity. While this land of today is vastly different to what he found, it may certainly be said of my experience that the American continues this tradition of association, more so than any other nation's men. The man here has a demonstrable civic zeal, of almost percolating quality; he is willing to make the time to take advantage of the political privileges bestowed upon him to ensure a favorable outcome for the entirety of his community. This sets him at a pronounced variance with the apathy of his Western counterparts. The choice of a Latin derivative for the name of the legislative assembly of this country is most apt—"congressus"—a reference to the active process of having come together. Even with this choice, this man carved his exceptionalism early, with the majority of other nations of the West favoring the nomenclature of "Parliament', a reference to a mere place of speech.

This nation is a republic, not a democracy; a most telling distinction and one that the hardest of men here like to impress. Unlike the numerous democratic forms of government of the West, where the outsider as an individual has no protection against the unlimited power of the majority, this man's form is a constitutionally limited government with the intent of controlling the majority to protect the individual's God-given and unalienable rights through a written Constitution. Religious liberty is the founding rock of democratic freedom and the man here understands this. To study and observe the formation of government here is to realize its main elements spring from the predominant Christian perspective.

In common parlance, a reference to the type of government, rather than the strict form of government, the American has a most enviable and outstanding democracy. He is a highly prejudiced man; prejudiced to the tenets of democracy and free will. One feels he must never be convinced to shed this deeply held prejudice; such a turn would relegate his land and people to moral and financial destitution. He appears aware that a nation requires just two generations of utopian statism before she incapacitates herself from recovery. I find that the American understands, to his great credit, that at its core, utopianism is profoundly anti-democratic. The American is quixotic yet fails to embrace utopian ideas; a most interesting paradox.

A Distrust of Government

The American has a most fervid, almost blazing distaste for and mistrust in government. He extols the virtues of the limited government at the drop of a hat; his dislike of big government reflex, a genetic within his makeup. He, I find almost uniformly, is acutely aware that the most deliberate choice of freedom over tyranny by his ancestry, and continued until modern times, has been altogether vindicated through his society's success. The fact that civil authorities are subject to several guidelines and limitations throughout Scripture is far from lost on the man here, again most relevant considering his religious character. This overriding commitment to a small government is augmented by concomitant beliefs in natural law, wealth creation and a sentiment of non-elitism. The man of this land, it can only be said, is fluent in the simple arithmetic of reality: with the growth of government, arrives the reduction of individual liberty. The only aristocracy existent in the society of this land is one grounded not on birth or need, but on individual courage, effort and vision. The American state has efficaciously farmed creativity and innovation by proffering enormous scope to the American in pursuit of these efforts. This scope, first envisioned by the founding fathers, is the ultimate characterization of the American republic and her people. Where the outsider feels limited or constrained by bureaucratic interference or the need for government approval, the American is dissimilarly empowered knowing success is not contingent on these but him. The man here, compared to his number in other lands, is the least servile I have ever known. Deference appears a foreign construct to the man and his land here. I find him also to be the least inclined of men to overbear on another man. Further, I find this man here to be the most politically nostalgic I have ever met; a classic mix of his emotions, patriotism and interest in political foundations.

I must conclude from all my sauntering of the streets here that the men of other lands cannot find finer endorsement of the merits of limited government than the experience of this experiment here. I find the American, aware that this is the major thread of his success tapestry, is unrestrained in his liberty; unlike the fierce cultural streak of utilitarianism that compels even the most obstinate outsider to surrender his individual liberty, no such ailment afflicts the American. The greatness of the American system lies in the nature of the man here; it would appear no political move in this country is deemed innocuous with suspicion leveled at each. He sees liberty not as illusory as the self-appointed intellectual guardian of the world today does but as the supreme value.

The man of this land understands that the government is a far worse employer than the private sector; that it cannot create net jobs, but most certainly can destroy them with regulation. His anchor is self-belief, family and faith; the outsider's, government. The jealous outsider would astonish at the satisfaction or elation of the American in his success or achievement, presumably quickly denigrating such displays as histrionics. The empathy of the outsider in these matters cannot be expected; he is accustomed only to an oversized and intrusive government serving as a permanent safety blanket. The size of government bears a direct correlation to the level of satisfaction in its citizens; if failure is not possible, pleasure in success suffers stark attenuation. Deep pleasure is the child of meaning and effort, and the government of great size eliminates this entire family. The American has the right view: nothing worthier exists than the glory of human accomplishment. The happiness of the man here springs from faith, vocation, community and family, all of which flower through the uniquely narrow ambit of the American government. A government with a narrow ambit fructifies a superior citizen; an intrusive government discharges the citizen from moral responsibility, spirituality, emotion and incentive to achievement. The emotional depth of the American is, I find, most noticeable; a trait absent in the outsider as no amount of easily accessible entertainment or pleasure can satisfy genuinely the human spirit. The American appears much more greatly devoted to his profession than the European, with the latter more dedicated to leisure and holidays, with the view of work as an unfortunate necessity. Many of the organizations of this country offer no mandatory retirement age, and a standard paid holiday period of fourteen days; a privilege earned only after a few years. The man here I find to belong to no one; unlike the average outsider whose identity is ascribed by nativity. The American's identity is the most malleable of things; a choice he makes. He is limited not by his cultural ancestry, or genetics, or the success of his parents; only by his imagination, heart and desire. He values productivity more than any other man; inaction or simply being is the sphere of the mediocre. This innate romance with productivity means the American is more likely to seek and earn his identity through his work; the unemployed or retired American, I discover to be a most forlorn sight, as the absence of work erodes the sense of worth, crucial to the psychology of the human.

A Traditional Life

The traversal of this nation reveals that the American still lives the most traditional life; an irony given his ingenuity, innovation and exceptional historical capacity for change he has demonstrated in virtually all spaces. The American continues to marry and raise a family, circumstances dissentient to the lives of the modern European and other Westerners. Children remain a central part of the American's life, averting the culture of self-absorption, rife in the outside world. The strong faith of the man here, I conclude, is preventative of these spiritual shortcomings that have befallen the outsider. The life of the American and his neighborhood feel drenched with reality, a departure from the contrived civility common in the outsider's neighborhoods. Life, birth, death, work, raising children, and helping neighbors compromise the everyday of this man's life; a textured life, of occasional tumult and delight. Through this currency of actuality, and charity, emerges the strongest of adhesive within a community. The great wonder of this culture is that within this realm of reality is the desire of upward mobility, distinct to the outsider's comparatively glossy life which seldom holds the target of greatness. The connection of the republican democracy with laissez faire economics first posited by the great Scottish pioneer of political economy, Adam Smith, is most alive in this great nation. It was the Frenchman outsider, de Tocqueville, who first noted that the American was unfazed at the proposition of people living in accordance only to their earning, at the mercy of the marketplace. Each individual should be gifted the opportunity to succeed economically without interference from the state; this is an ideal to which I find this man to be most committed. The greatest capitalist alive, the American, through this commitment, has etched his society with hard work, upward mobility, equal opportunity and individuality. The connection between Christianity and capitalism is telling;

the work ethic of the man of this land largely shaped by the Protestant influence ensures economic invigoration. Just as the low taxation of the citizen is paramount to his success, reduced government spending is essential to the health of the finances of a nation. The American is fierce in his protection of his property; he has most minimal patience for the government that violates his rights in this regard.

The conviction in individual action is connubial with individual responsibility. Any attempt to nullify responsibility of the individual by transfer to the collective is savaged by the American, met with ferocity without equal. The transuding exceptionalism of the man here is amassed through, and predicated on, a forced self-improvement dependency. Self-reliance is the great nemesis of the powerful government; this is why the American is resolute in his obstruction of matters pertaining to socialized healthcare, housing assistance and unemployment benefits. The values of the American are wholly disputatious with these programs; where others see human rights, he sees privilege.

The man here has an irrepressible fixation on the future, commensurate with and companionable to, his optimism. He appears neither stoic nor resigned to any particular fate; he considers destiny a destination of his own choosing, a position which, at first blush, is inconsistent with his belief in God's plan for him. I find the man here to be a doer and most moderate in his patience for the individual of little activity, particularly the intellectual. There is in the atmosphere of the American life a swirling wind of mistrust and antipathy of the intellectual elite, and their political gravitation. It is inconceivable that the political aspirant of this land with doctorate qualification would publicly adopt his academic title. The American intellectual, utilizing his education in practical, tangible and pragmatic context is, however, a welcome contribution.

Improvisation and adaptation are the key tools of the American workshop; the contingency of change ever ready in its top shelf. This man here, most unbending in a great many matters, would appear a greatly improbable candidate for change yet history and my observation is otherwise suggestive. This is because the American, in the face of struggle, equates change to a successful future. No finer lateral thinker exists than the American; this outstanding ability never failing to amaze in velocity and volume. The apparatus of change and lateral thought, accompanied by self-belief steeped in the Christian faith, when operating in harmony, shelter this man from permanent political, economic and social debacle. These are the conclusions drawn by the outsider of the seemingly infallible American, exhibitive throughout his history of an extraordinary capacity for the realignment of the national trajectory, however imminent. The most notable of change illustrations was the American's response to domestic education in the wake of the Soviet launch of Sputnik; the culmination of which was a comprehensive whipping by the National Aeronautics and Space Administration (NASA) of the Russians. It was again de Tocqueville who first beheld these unique and exceptional capabilities. And it is today perhaps the time that the American, one feels, would benefit most from a major collective and national achievement of similar proportion.

The autonomous American does, on occasion seek leadership or resolution, and when doing so; unlike the outsider his impulse is local, not federal or central. The states of this man are sovereign; an intentional endeavor framed by the magnificent Constitution, to balance the power of the central authority. His federalism is enormously exceptional in and of itself; the indispensable machinery of the grand American Republic here. The system of the American is most flexible, amid enormous variation among state jurisdictions in laws and regulations. It is striking that the European and his Union find great pride in their diversity yet are most intractable in their approach to legislative discrepancy among member nations. It is to be said, of course, that the exceptional democracy is the one permitting of the greatest flexibility.

Politics and Ideology

The political system of the American is truly a sight to behold; the landscape enough to excite any man's lust. Inspiration, individuality, independence and opportunity are the flavors of the political ice cream. The outsider bleeds in disappointment at his political choices and weeps tears of pessimism for his democracy. The American, it must be said, is always upbeat, believing that his ballot and those of his fellow patriots can and will affect any change desired by them. The political style is charismatic, not transactional; the struggle of genuine ideas and philosophical difference still alive here unlike in the lands of England and Australia. It is, I conclude, this man's optimism that has ensured he has not embraced the transactional politics of purely management and finance in the other lands of English speakers; the philosophical fight and culture war rages here as man believes and is optimistic he can win hearts and minds, refusing to accept the view that man cannot be changed.

The man of this proud nation is addicted to the genuinely free election by the people periodically. He puts up propositions and almost every position available in his society for election almost interminably; from the school board to the drain commissioner to the town dog catcher. The Western outsider is unaccustomed to this all-encompassing breadth and regularity of election; in his lands, the police force, the local school, the hospital, the cemetery, the waste collection and all such matters are the territory of the bureaucrat, with most limited oversight by the politician. These decentralized democratic traditions of today were those that de Tocqueville so admired; the hurdles to tyranny. The American seems to me, as I traipse through the wide main streets of angular parking in his smaller towns, to have always understood that government can only do him, his culture and his community harm if it is able to reach him; this is why he has always insisted on voting for his judges, his police and his schools. The localization of power is his mechanism of defense, I find. The free outsider sees only the ballot for his political representative and the most occasional referendum; he falsely convinces himself that this is sufficient to satisfy the criterion of democracy. His failure, it must be said, is that he either does not understand or care that within these circumstances, the individual is still easily dislodged or sequestered. It is here that the exceptionalism of the civic pride of the American saves him; he remains largely, as in de Tocqueville's day, unwilling to compromise his sovereignty, comprehending the futility of the individual vote in the presence of the all-powerful government. The man here parades a great animus toward the bureaucrat, regarding him a force of individual liberty dismemberment and a significant impairment to his pursuit of happiness. The outsider finds striking the American's unblurred and categorical position; as with the great man of all nations, he desires to be represented, not governed.

Exceptional America

The threshold of man's liberty is his choice to cast a vote; without it, the democratic system is little but a hollow roar, an affront to the cost of blood and treasure sacrificed by men. Many of the outsider's countries compel him by law to vote, with the looming threat of financial penalty, gnawing at the soul of his liberty. The American volunteers his vote, within a salubrious voluntary voting system reciprocating of the freedom on which it is constituted. The outcomes of the system are patently espousing of the American culture; independence, individuality, risk, optimism, opportunity, meritocracy and freedom. These ends are achieved in this land through the presence of the genuine political movement, the culture of giving, the eminence of the policy institute; the primary election and the medley of free and unfettered opinion. In all matters of politics, across each theatre, the individual of this nature is elevated to levels elusive of the ravenous wolves of the collective.

The collectivist, in spite of his withered hand, wields his ideology, casting an enormous shadow on the political process of his county. The outsider is consequentially home to nations of which the political discourse is most meager; the battlefield of the political game exclusive to the apathetic, unaligned centre, particularly in those with the mandatory vote. With ears attuned to an entirely different siren, the American system is calculatingly colorful, presenting a smorgasbord of conjecture and debate. The American when casting his vote, faithful to his philosophy, does so for an individual; whereas the outsider, forever in the collectivist mindset, votes for an individual based on his team. The elected representatives and general party members of the outsider's political culture are subject to the fevered dreams of the collectivist: ownership through party discipline and the creation of the monolithic block. This absurd notion, formed on the most brittle of glass, produces an environment most inhospitable to the individual; he is unable to freely express the opinion, dissentient to party policy, without fear of retribution or punishment. The individual, defiant of these parameters, is pilloried and persecuted by the media and establishment alike; branded a cowboy or rogue or maverick or renegade, and derided for a lack of team play. The maverick here, I find with great delight, is not marginalized or expelled in the pursuit of success; in fact, he is embraced and honored for traits indicative of leadership quality. In the Westminster system of the British and Australian, a representative crossing the floor is a crisis; to this man, it is simply another day. The American system, I feel it must be said, is a cacophony of voices; the outsider's a robotic machine where a convergence of ideas, set by a select few, controls the tone for the country. When one of the chief vehicles—the political party—of democracy is prohibitive of free speech, it is most anemic.

The American is the most ideological of men. He, on both sides of the political equation, is a natural disseminator of news and ideas, sparking an acute and alert citizenry. With customary flamboyance, resourcefulness and dualism, the American through political activism has exceptionally sired myriad outlets and organizations, of an online, corporate, not-for-profit and media nature, for commentary and analysis. These outlets function in tandem with an ideological movement, and with all the cunning and dexterity of the finest private-sector economy successes. The system of this man, of immeasurable superiority to the system of the outsider, largely supplants the political party with the political, ideological grassroots movement. The political ardor of the American rests with the movement and its unadulterated purity of principle; the committed

Republican voter, for example, is a Christian first, then an American, then a conservative, and then a Republican. Support for the major party is therefore hardly automatic. The elected representative of the American is largely answerable to a seemingly omnipotent and uncompromising ideological movement, not a centralized bureaucratic office of a party. Indeed the American harbors a degree of unsmiling suspicion in relation to the elites of the political party, including the silver haired and tongued politician of too many years; a result of the political party's dilution of principle, bastardisation of hodgepodge ideas and culture of compromise. I note with interest, that the man here departs from his desire for the individual in the behavior of his politician, not unlike the outsider. He takes great umbrage at even the effective and charming elected representative the moment they perceive him to display individual traits of ornery, expecting them to conduct themselves in a collective manner—not politically, but behaviorally. The man here has displayed immunity to his Western peers who have sought a path of racing to the middle, or mediocrity; his politics instead remain most passionate and divergent to his opponents; partisanship most rare. These realities, along with the aptitude of the American for quick and powerful organization and association, makes this man a most unlikely candidate for being taken for granted. The conservative American understands far better than his counterpart in the outside world that the preaching of the Left urging civility is their effort to silence criticism through the disparagement of the detractor, as ignorant or extreme.

The American is also the most political of men; the visitor taken aback at the openness of the American in declaring political allegiance. This is a society at great odds with the modern; it is not yet betrothed to the moderated and balanced approaches of consensus and compromise; that is to say, there are many men here that oppose or support with passion that would be spoken of as fanatics in other lands. It is for this reason, I believe, that the elites of this nation may never find a natural habitat, unable to camouflage their actions and deride the detractor by suggestion he is out of sync with the rational mode of thinking. It would seem such an environment prevents the genuine fanaticism of the elite. It is, of course, without the slightest of doubt that the cultural foundation of the free and open polity is owed entirely to the Judeo-Christian traditions. This is a matter I find that clearly the man here understands, and I can only determine it is why this man clings most strongly to his traditions; his religious character and devotion to freedom is the savior of his traditions.

Negotiation and settlement of political differences appear most scarce in the contemporary times of this nation. The man here, I find, picks a side; the middle considered a most unbecoming location, an almost permanent cultural war. Partisan rancor is most common, but unlike in the nations of other men, it leaves little evidence of paralysis. Passion is such here that the visitor traveling through this land finds it rare to find a husband and wife, one Republican and the other Democratic. The American father frowns on the daughter courting a man of a different political persuasion or belonging to a family of such disposition. Such considerations appear far earlier in the line of questioning of the parent than they would in the outsider nations. These matters deepen the political chasm, encouraging cultural and political homogeneity.

A policy more adversative to the American founding, culture and experience than affirmative action is beyond imagination; the American is correspondingly powerless in concealing or curtailing his utter contempt. He recoils in horror at the legislative underpinning of purportedly progressive and inclusive equity programs, believing most dynamically in the best man for the job; that merit trump all else. The political parties of the countries of the outsider often employ formal affirmative action; setting gender and ethnic quotas, ensuring a certain number of individuals of a specific type must stand for election. Opportunity is a most illimitable concept to the man who calls himself an American. His system, while imperfect, is the most perfect of any, it must be said and I can only conclude. At its best, on a political level, the American is delivered a rigorous meritocracy, rewarding of talent, performance and risk. The man here is astonished to learn that their primary election system, one of the exceedingly few helpful outcomes of the progressivism early in the twentieth century, is completely unique to them. The outsider, who would rather be spared the disruption of another election, leaves the process of selection to a small, select group, inclusive of bureaucrats, of a political party. The fate of the nomination and potential contribution rests not with that individual or the broader populace but a small group of establishment elites. In accordance with the American's view on individuality and opportunity, the primary system to be found here is the most exceptional process of selection in the world, affording any aspirant the chance to prove their worthiness. The qualities of leadership, communication and charisma are secondary in the appraisal of the outsider political aspirant; of more concern is his disposition to acquiescence and indisposition to boldness with conviction, thus making him a most manageable and welcome addition.

The prospect of term limiting elected representatives is one which tears at the soul of the American; a brutal contest between the illimitability of individual opportunity and liberty, and a utilitarian inclination driven by patriotism seeking the betterment of the nation. This is the only time, visible to the outsider, where individual liberty and opportunity writhe in genuine vulnerability. While the American is quick to lament the quality of his elected representatives and the emergence of the career politician, it is again a matter of his nation falling behind his potential; the elected politicians of America are truly exceptional in talent, ability and communication, compared to their Western equivalents. It is not uncommon for this man to possess a general dislike, or even resentment, of the political profession; in fact it is in many parts, most likely. Unlike the equivalent antipathy for the politician held by the outsider shrouded in envy, the American's is a result of the location of sovereignty in his political system, coupled with his resolve to thwart the concentration of power. This man is most unlikely to be interested in the expenses or resources available to the political representative, funded by the taxpayer; a glaring contrast to the public scrutiny, ongoing commentary and vicious criticism of the outsider of any and every sweetener in the politician's life. The finely veined marble and opulence of the American's Capitol is considered a most fitting tribute.

The Architect of the American Dream

Office often holds little charm for the man here, I find, in that it must often be purchased at the sacrifice of his conscience and the loss of his self-respect. The people of this country, I must tell you, are a tide no force can resist for a prolonged period. If faced with the prospect of being ostracized, the American is most happy, should the alternative be to submit to usurpation. He is often tendered gratuitously taunts yet he submits to them without any disposition of unkindness or imputation. He is often charged by the outsider for reasons of his culture as disposed to racism and sexism yet it is the American that has, with success, in comparison to the men of other lands, ensured opportunity for the educated and ambitious African American and woman. For all the commitment to the principles of good constitutionally limited government, the conservative American must always remember that that strong and effective government can and has enhanced the nation of America.

The conservative American has been the architect of the American dream, and great governance has played its role in ensuring the American formula remains intact. The American has been assured until now in that his state has, unlike others, advanced human liberty. The man here understands the role of his state in eliminating polio in his children and protecting the great wilderness areas of Yellowstone and Yosemite with national parks. This is, without question, the most libertarian land of them all, but it is a natural component of the man here, I find, not his ideology. I consider the man with the ideology of the libertarian as most defective but the man with the natural libertarian disposition the most superior of men. The American may be more disposed to the libertarian streak than any other man but he must be careful, for any journey to the land of the libertarian and his territories of anarchy will surely be his last.

Nick Adams

Armed

The American faces a violent criticism, embraced with well-nigh unanimity by all the outsiders of his borders; his right to keep and bear arms, as enshrined in his Second Amendment of his magnificent Constitution. This nation with its abundant affluence in the military, economic, scientific and cultural dominions is prodigious; the disputing man of grand delusion and suffering the emerald corrosion of envy. The outsider, therefore, destitute in liberty and armed by his socialistic masters with collectivist and politically correct proclivities from a young age clings to the gun culture of this country as evidence of his moral and cultural superiority over the American. The control of the firearm by the governments of the outside world is further cosmetic in their already feminized operations; with the exception of America in the Western world, the gun is considered to deserve no role in life. The owner or advocate of the gun in these cultures is considered the most uncouth and offensive of men; branded a Neolithic or Neanderthal, he is most prone to derision, scorn, belittlement and ostracizing by his fellow outsiders. The outsider proclaims the absence of guns in his society with a straight face; a gunless society is not of existence, the criminals of the outsider's country will most certainly possess them. The coalition of firearm control and the reality of criminal ownership materialize the most portentous of circumstances: a society in which the criminal is armed, and the law-abiding citizen is unarmed. These realities presciently explained by the words of the famous American of Presidential and authorial note, Thomas Jefferson,

> Laws that forbid the carrying of arms . . . disarm only those who are neither inclined nor determined to commit crimes . . . such laws make things worse for the assaulted and better for the assailants; they serve rather to encourage than to prevent homicides, for an unarmed man may be attacked with greater confidence than an armed man.

The American is more cognizant of any that the absence of his Second Amendment renders redundant his other Amendments; that the remainder of the most imitated admired and long-standing document of modern history is relegated to all the paltriness and feebleness of the recommendation. He is a most sapient student of history, conscious that the first act of every totalitarian regime of the last century was the disarmament of the regular citizenry. An unarmed population is inutile in any contest between it and government; the ripest of produce for the big government farmer. The great Jefferson again:

> The strongest reason for people to retain the right to keep and bear arms is, as a last resort, to protect themselves against tyranny in government.

This is embossed in the psyche of the American and his culture. It is for these fears, embossed in his and the national psyche, the famed spirited vigilance in the preservation of his Second Amendment Rights exists in this man. The disarmament of the civilian is premised in the irresponsibility and distrust of the citizen, unless employees of the government; an antipodal opposition to the premise of the founding of the American nation: an inclination to suspect the government, not the people.

The subterranean disdain of the man of this land for the large and intrusive government is the most unbreakable of granite pillars in American cultural support for the right to bear arms. The outsider, injected with the infective trifecta of freedom—illiteracy, collectivism, and dislike of the American, is incapable of understanding the sentiment. The Western outsider practices an impure freedom; a precarious tightrope walk neutralizing freedom to and freedom from. The authenticity of the freedom of this great land dictates an almost exclusive practice of freedom to. It is why the American lives in the land of extremes; this is what freedom and scale of population brings. This individualistic land flourishes individuals and innovation. The American is the only man who offers the individual antecedence to society. The eclipse of individual freedom is insuperable; a state the others of the First World with their collectivist diathesis are unable to comprehend and unwilling to entertain. This diathesis means the abode of the Western outsider is gorged with the foods of effeminacy, decadence and marshmallow fluff. This diet of the outsider results in the addiction of government welfare dialysis and cowed masses in the blind obey of the dictates of government. This exigency is most unconducive to the presence of the firearm. The American views his government with rightful suspicion; the outsider with reverence befitting the church.

The right to bear arms is a centerpiece of the American's exceptionalism; synonymous with freedom. The flag of freedom flies with a permanent gust of wind: the puissant blowing breath of the American. While generating the sorest of chafes between the thighs of the politically correct and big government elites that litter the world, it is a most true assertion that a man without a gun is a captain without a ship. This natural state of man has been under steady fire from such elites, who have armed the sheep of their nations with the ammunition of falsehood. The outsider is today as a result is abounding in the preponderant sentiment that the firearm is most unnecessary; a tool of the bad for much evil. The outsider of most countries consider government controls or restrictions of the firearm are not only rightful, but of necessity. The truth of the firearm has been majorly distorted in the non-American society. The actuality is that the right to bear arms is the greatest test of the genuineness of freedom; the best protection of the individual, his family and his property; the greatest deterrent to governmental overreach; the greatest disincentive against foreign invasion and the greatest asset to a confident and individualistic society. The American is most incisive in these matters, acutely aware of the realities and bereft of complacency.

Where the remote prospect or threat of personal harm or inconvenience has the outsider willing to sign away any liberty; the American is mulish. He surprises in the conjecture and surrounding expostulation in that his Second Amendment codifies his fundamental, God-given individual right to keep and bear arms. It must be said that the major cities of America are a most different equation to the towns that are the heartbeat of the American nation; their restrictions on the firearm are not as onerous as the outsider's but close to.

The ubiquity of the firearm right across this land overawes the outsider; it feels that the man here has sufficient number to arm his entire population twice over. The right of the American to bear arms not only ensures the circumspection of the federal government but a shot in the arm flooding the veins of international enemies with fear. There is absolutely no uncertainty this nation may ever be overcome by means of physical invasion, as enunciated by the Commander-in-Chief of the Imperial Japanese Navy during the Second World War, Isoroku Yamamoto:

> You cannot invade the mainland United States. There would be a rifle behind every blade of grass.

The American, I find to be, part of a most effective militia; that of the individual private citizen. The invasion of other nations could occur with the barest of fire-fights; a nation vanquished most quickly.

The outsider is startled to learn that the women and elderly of the American nation are as likely, if not more so, to keep and bear firearms, and provide the greatest advocacy for the Second Amendment. In the quintessential American mercantile spirit, the gun has become a fashion accessory, with detailed decorative color and flair, designed for the use of the American woman. The American child is most likely to own a Daisy Red Ryder; a toy considered an illegal firearm by the outsider's nations. The older American is empowered, as the female American is, by the firearm.

The American believes in the self-defense right of the individual; an ability of him to protect himself, his family and property. It is true that the American may have more sympathy for the vigilante than the outsider, although the outsider often wrongly considers mere self-defense tantamount to vigilantism. The preservation of individual liberty is at the forefront of the American mindset. The American must continue to be wary; even the fellow frontier nation of Australia to which this outsider belongs has forsaken her rugged individualism and self-determination, submitting to the dictates of government and surrendering the right and advantage of being armed, once an inconceivable proposition. The tumors of the great cancers of socialism and radical Islam in the United States are until now largely benign; the arming of the American a most effectual deterrent.

The outsider is stunned at the great numbers of people of the citizenry of this nation that readily explain that upon the election of the last President, they immediately went to their gun stores to purchase more weaponry and ammunition. This indication of the nature of the American and the lengths he travels to protect the freedom and liberty so vigorously fought for by his forefathers leaves little doubt: the American is a truly exceptional being.

Chapter 9
IMPERILED

The American, I find to be, at this time most unsettled; his famed optimism on the wane. He is sharply cognizant that the outsider considers this to be the Chinese century; an element of the broader world opinion that the finest days of the American nation are a matter of history. The American, a man of scant acquaintance with the outside world cannot compare himself to the outsider but nevertheless involuntarily senses the national awry. This is most unfamiliar terrain for the American, a man accustomed to chartering only the most exceptional of waters from birth. He today struggles to remember a time when his beloved country was not the lion nation of the world zoo. Despite his great unease, insecurity and economic ache, the mind of the American rightfully disbelieves the materialization of his greatest fears. The literati of the world do not obfuscate their hatred of this land; their voices an organized chorus singing joyously the predictions of the post-American world in unison. But the disconnect of the literati with the everyday person is famed; I must say as I stand here on its soil, the American nation most certainly feels most unlike a nation in decline, or the sufferer of sweeping malaise.

Exceptional America

The mere mention of the American economy has always in days past instantly puffed the American chest with pride, but today instead drains the color from his face. The unprecedented magnitude of his national debt is a source of immense distress for the man here; the situation most lacking in sustainability and tenure. I find him to be clearly affected by the neighbor or member of his church congregation not in employ, a situation of increasing incidence, and one for which he often weeps.

It is true of any nation that the nucleus of national power rests with the national economy; a battered economy is a strained power, always wrestling. But much like her story the American economy is exceptional, for she is undergirded by impregnable material: the opaque steel of military power and the unshakeable cement of technological advantage. The debt of the American that has him wiping the sweat off his brow does not inhibit his key capability: to be the driving influence on global markets. He is largely buffered by his ability to print the world's premier reserve currency and the perception held by the outside world in spite of the arithmetical reality. Only the most calamitous of wars could realign international influence based on economics one would imagine. This is not to discount or downplay the albatross that hangs around the man of this land's neck: a public and private debt burden totaling an amount almost four times the size of gross domestic product is unsustainable, perilous and unforgivable. Of greater concern to this man than his debt ratio is the interest rates on new debt that the investor may demand, should perceptions change, complicating any recovery and potentially assassinating the economy here with brutality.

The American, the most confident and forthright of men, is a curious study in insecurity, often greatly discounting of his historical malleability and resulting rejection of imminent submersion. In him, I find to lie a most miraculous and unique faculty: the lifting or clearing of the densest of miasmas. This phenomenon was first identified by the genius of the twenty-seven-year-old de Tocqueville with his pithy illumination:

> The greatness of America lies not in being more enlightened than any other nation, but rather in her ability to repair her faults.

It must be said that I consider this man they call the American to be disposed of a most boomerang of natures; a resilient population committed to not just survival but preservation of exceptionalism. He has endured dreary leadership on the home-front and hostile aggression abroad; not even the coarsest of economic times whether recession or depression or the demands of civil and foreign war on multiple occasions has more than temporarily disoriented and hindered him. He is much like his invention; a Kevlar man.

The great former Prime Minister of England, Winston Churchill once surmised socialism as the "philosophy of failure, the creed of ignorance, and the gospel of envy." The defects of failure, ignorance, and envy are a vehement antithesis; most anathematic to the life and culture that I find to exist here of the American. The absences of these matters that wilt the personality and constrain the heart mean that the American is most unversed in the dogma of socialism; bureaucrats, leftists, collectivists, statists and progressives are the axis of the enemies of this man.

The Threat of China

The man of outside lands is likely most swift to foretell the advance of the Chinese. It is with irony I note that perhaps the greatest advice for the American of today comes from the Chinese symbol for the word crisis, comprising two words: danger and opportunity. Opportunity rarely arrives without danger; the American is more capable than any man to defeat his threats and emerge as he has in previous dangers stronger than ever. He must, I feel, return each inch of his soil to opportunity for the innovator or entrepreneur; to replicate what Cape Canaveral in the state of Florida did for the space program. He need only focus on himself; the great Chinese bully will suffer the same fate as those nations before him. He may threaten economically and geopolitically at this time but no nation can sustain success without granting its citizens economic and political liberty; the Chinese with all the money will always be a poor man's American; his denial of liberty always rendering him but a bootlace on the American shoe. Less than five percent of the Chinese have God as an important feature of their life; it will only be when Bibles and Churches appear in overwhelming and omnipresent number in China that the American may have a genuine competitor.

It may well be true the Chinese are exhibiting to some degree the traditional drive and pride of the American and only a fool would deny his growing economic prowess. But the view of the Chinese, I must say, as the inevitable inheritor of global superpower ignores his perils; a demographic gender imbalance as a result of the one-child policy, the great likelihood of social unrest and the growing political will of a rising middle class, assisted by technology which flattens the earth and allows mobilization and organization. The American, in dealing with the avalanche of prediction pertaining to the ascent of red China must not lose perspective. He should also remember the false claims of inevitability of the prowess of the Japanese economy a quarter of a century ago, and the fate of many other nations of communism.

An Almost Treasonous Culture War

The subjugation of danger is reliant upon accurate assessment and identification; not a time for posturing. The dangers for the American when listed in topical order, I conclude, include the malignant cancer of political correctness; statist ambition, epitomized best by current governmental overreach, seeking to replicate a European system of social democracy; the transformation of the classroom to the desires of bureaucratic elites; cultural relativism with the warm embrace of the Western approach of failed multiculturalism, the objective and intrinsic sinful action of abortion, homosexual marriage, and the rise of the Islamic, in the context of world history. I feel this man must be both priestly and prophetic, swiveling his neck to the other nations of the world to save himself from the errors of his fellow humanity. He must observe the demography of the European, and note the cultural prejudices and character dispositions of the outsider; for prejudices can override humanistic sentiment in a heartbeat. He must reject what perhaps first begun with President Roosevelt; an ambition for a different America, with public institutions that the great Alexis de Tocqueville would today find unrecognizable and of eminent disappointment.

The man here must identify that significant cultural change is neither instant nor achieved in one deft move; such change is only ever achieved gradually. The men of the other nations of the world were not always endowed with the steady erosion of values that besiege them today. Instead, as an unwary frog in a pot of candy-coated social democratic cold water distortions, he was slowly boiled to his fate. Were he aware of his potential fate, much like a frog placed in boiling water, the European, the Australian, the Canadian and the Brit, would almost certainly have refused to begin the process. It is difficult for the visitor to judge if the American and his famed resistance is still outside the cooking utensil of the secular elite, or whether the American has entered with the heating being slowly applied by him. Such judgment is difficult because once more, it is a case of the American falling behind his own potential, not that of any other nation. The American, in either scenario, benefited by the historical experience of others, has before him the clearest course: to not enter the pan, or to jump out immediately.

The secular elite have a growing voice in this land, I find; they by no means are the pulse of the American wrist, but their middling and meddlesome efforts through the radio, television, newspaper, classroom and lecture hall, do capture his ears. These elites wish to perform dramatic surgery on the American heart, such that the surgery would render him unrecognizable. The ever-creeping well-worn and familiar catalogue of clichés, accompanied with the concealing burka of political correctness, remind the visitor of his own nation, or others. Designed at removing the furniture of confidence and the rug of exceptionalism in the American living room, these political and cultural elites motivated by a fraudulent secular moral superiority, paint the nation deceitfully, using not one lick of red, white and blue.

The American must take heed at this time, most closely of the famous Roman philosopher and orator, Cicero:

> A nation can survive its fools, and even the ambitious. But it cannot survive treason from within. An enemy at the gates is less formidable, for he is known and carries his banner openly. But the traitor moves amongst those within the gate freely, his sly whispers rustling through all the alleys, heard in the very halls of government itself. For the traitor appears not a traitor; he speaks in accents familiar to his victims, and he wears their face and their arguments, he appeals to the baseness that lies deep in the hearts of all men. He rots the soul of a nation, he works secretly and unknown in the night to undermine the pillars of the city, he infects the body politic so that it can no longer resist. A murderer is less to fear.

He must, I feel, exercise enormous wariness to the actions of those within that wittingly or unwittingly seek to prosper those without.

The Malady of Political Correctness

The American must wage the most decimating of battles against the malady of political correctness; dancing with the spirit of an unconquered foe, her malignancy is unchecked in the other lands. Vociferously promoted by the media and academic elite, it is the stovepipe of the anti-American chimney. A device of the cabal of the atheistic misanthropic, the censorious and irrational system consigns even the most obdurate to the vacillating. A brainchild of illiberal liberals, the framework of political correctness, I find it threatens greatly the American and his objectives, in both the homeland and internationally. In the creed of the politically correct, features among others, that competition, save for sport, is of moral question as it promotes inequality; Islam a religion of peace; all cultures of equal rank or value; wealth a matter of guilt, save for the athlete or entertainer; the nation state an outdated model; Christian, Western civilization primarily accountable for poverty and all deficiencies in the world; not only do all people have equal rights, everyone is equal and; conditions of life are a matter of circumstance, not choice.

The politically correct and statist ambitions of domestic forces imperil the exceptionalism of the man here; I am left with no doubt. The traditions of opportunity, liberty, freedom, hard work and entrepreneurship are the building blocks of the culture and politics of the American. These are not merely inimical to socialistic principles, but render this great land the great conservative nation: the penultimate citadel of anti-socialism. This is why the American elicits the hatred of the outsider, conditioned in collectivism and baptized in socialistic water.

Taxation and a Disdain for Bailouts

The American today repels viciously the governmental overreach most reminiscent of the framework of European government, which has decapitated the limbs of populations of the nations of the continent. It is not a matter for denial that the government of this man has engaged in takeover and bailout in recent history; actions of renunciation of the traditions of the American model. Matters of limited government have appeared lost even in the administrations of conservative politics; a matter which should be, and appears to be, of measureless concern to the man here, and a prognosis of situation. Nothing less than the optimism of this man is at stake; he need only look at the law and regulation in the Western nations to understand the thick gloom that besets them. Excessive law and regulation quench not only the capacity, but the joy of man, squelching his fun.

The American belongs to a nation to which there is no worthy comparison. In him, carries this man, I find everywhere I go, a most discernible sharpness; a noteworthy hunger redolent of an almost near desperation delivering a diacritic mettle. It is this mental build that sees the man here the most competitive and innovative of all men. In this sprawling land, the absence of the government ballast not just allows man the ultimate nobility of freedom but mandates him to conduct his affairs and perform his duties to optimal capacity, for no less than the livelihood of his children could rest upon it. The intensity of these conditions has been the engine of the exceptionalism in science, military, economy and technology. Insecurity is the most titanic of inducement, and the American finds a native interdependence with it. The amelioration of this insecurity or vacation of these conditions which would amount to the replication of the failed European welfare model would render, I have no doubt, this man a mere clone of the outsider; thieving him his individualistic instinct and expunging his voracious appetite. This is tantamount to the nullification of exceptionalism and the castration of the American. The American with a steady eye on his founding is ever cognizant of these repercussions of mediocrity and laments the ebbing in checks and balances of the government; he waits impatiently to restore these matters by casting his vote. Irony is most perpetual in the life of this man, it must be said: the insecurity of the American is premised on the least insecure, and most admirable and profound of beliefs: that man can achieve without the assistance of government.

An individual within any society which has had the nuclear family as its primary cultural norm throughout history, much like the English-speaking civilization, is most curtailed in his sense of entitlement and expectation from and of the state. He lives a dynamic existence: free to choose whom he wishes to marry and when he shall leave home; he relies not on the broader family but is in ownership of his own life. While the outsider of the developed world is today encased with these liberties, these are often newfound, hardly time-honored. The genetics of a culture steep in origin and tradition. They dispense indelible psychological indentation to the individual; a mode of thinking unable to be bested, even in the wake of fresh liberty. The American suffers no such affliction; from a young age he is made to understand his life will be carved of his own hands and he must be prepared to journey companionless. As he starts his own family, he becomes more detached from his greater family unlike the European, conceding further protection and assistance; a further reason for this man's known electricity and force in matters of career and financial prosperity. It is these cultural genetics, attributive to the individualist nuclear family structure, that emancipate the man here and bathe his subconscious with self-reliance.

While it is true that all manner of men submit their money to tax reluctantly; I find this man to be the most ill-disposed of all men to taxation. A new tax triggers immediate altercation between the American and the responsible governmental authority; a joust that almost never ends in grudging acceptance, as it may in the more stiff-necked and individual outsider.

Encroachment of Islam

The once great nations of Europe, including the magnificent island of England, are inert matter: complacent, divest of God, individuality, responsibility and national pride. Her demography is shiftless; a fire fed by her lack of spirituality, insatiable appetite for political correctness, and the immigration of people of inferior culture and ability, audaciously unwilling to integrate into the host nation culture. Feminism is her aortic aneurysm, delivering her and Western civilization straight to the hands of the Islamic. The debt of many European countries is parlous; the collapse of the European market appearing imminent. The astute American rightly sees the absurdity in the pursuit of a European model. The solutions of the matters that cause enormous unrest to him are American; they lie not in the anti-individual and godless models of overseas territories of other continents. The outsider would be most wise to eschew thirstily his collectivism and dependence on the state; it is, without question or reticence, the American model to which all other nations must aspire to progress and preserve human civilization.

The American must remember that cultural superiority is tangible matter, measured by objective scales. All human beings are equal, but not all cultures are equal. No culture is without flaw, but some are better than others. While any member of the elite class may howl his protest, such illogical socialistic rumination must fall on deaf ears. Even the castle of such rumination, the United Nations, uncharacteristically awards a Human Development Index Ranking, using a serious of measurements such as GDP per capita, literacy, life expectancy, women's rights, and strength of democracy. To insist, as the relativist does that the culture of the Western nation ensuring equality before the law and freedom of speech bears no differentiation to the culture overseeing female genital mutilation, forced marriages and honor killings, is most reprehensible. The cultural relativist is the husband of the bureaucratic internationalist; the desirer of the weakening of the nation-state to create the body that governs for many. The bastard children of this illicit marriage are the edicts of multiculturalism and affirmative action; responsible for creating special interest groups and incentivizing membership of them through empowerment, while ushering a new ago of hostility. Assimilation to the members of these groups is only educating themselves of their new nation's weaknesses and the processes by which they may capitalize on these. The nation that advances that every culture is equal must expect new immigrants and new generations of previous immigrants to find little need for patriotism or loyalty.

The religion of the Islamic, when obeyed with inflexibility and literalness, and with an adherence to strictures, is a perpetual act of vandalism visited upon the ideals of the Western world, and one which will ultimately threaten the existence of America. The qualities deceptively adorned to the religion of Islam, most notably the ambition of peace, by the politically correct outsider are misplaced; it is the

Western world, beaconed by the American and his fellow English-tongued cousins across the oceans, that has sought peace. All theology is political; it has a bearing on the events of the process of politics. The American must jettison the urging for diplomacy, noting the pages of history, and the events lining them, in dealing with the germinating struggle against the radical Islamist, of either militant or stealth form. From the seventh century, for a period of almost 1400 years, the Islamist has fought to conquer alternative civilization; from the Battle of Tours in 732 to the Siege of Constantinople in 1453 to the Battle of Lepanto in 1571 to the Battle of Vienna in 1683. The Islamist, his actions and aspirations of today, are not representative of a contorted Islam as the secular elites may proclaim; to the contrary, they clearly follow the teachings of the Koran, within which lie the Hadith and the Sura. The American should apprise himself of the teachings of the Wahhabism developed in the eighteenth century and the workings of the leaders of the Muslim Brotherhood to orient himself, assess and decide his future action.

For the survival of the American, he should consider irrelevant the stillborn supposition of the elite outsider that no words critical of the Islamic faith be uttered, for the consequences are the inciting of hatred. The American must, as a matter for the continued health and unity of his nation, deafeningly and without the hint of hesitation, roar his opinion. Idolatry is not only the worship of wrong Gods, but the worship of God wrong. Tied to idolatry is a misplaced affection; a disorder. Islamic theology brings dishonor to God in that it worships the right God wrongly, tantamount to worshipping the wrong God.

He must reject the cultural, political and intellectual bully that is the radical Islamist of stealth persuasion. Ensuring restless sleep for both the American and any friend of his, attuned to the trends of Islamic immigrant populations within their own countries, is the unshakeable conclusion that, while still a minority within those that describe themselves as such, some Islamic Americans are beginning to exhibit the behavior of their counterparts in Europe and Australia. The last three years have borne witness to the events of Fort Hood, the revelation of the existence of several prominent anti-American Muslim leaders, the strategic depositing of Sharia Law as a matter of public debate, and the accusations of persecution and the demand for increased cultural sensitivity toward their practices. The brazen push for an Islamic prayer centre to be located on the site of the former World Trade Center, or in its close vicinity, is a flashing alert sign of the brightest color that the waters of American tolerance are being subjected to test and provocation.

The recognition of Sharia Law in Western democracies is perhaps the most visible and pressing imperative for the Islamist. The American, the man with the greatest appreciation of the liberties of Western democracy recoils in horror at the strictures of Sharia Law. This unfathomable quest for recognition is sponsored by the deformity of thought and action by the secular elites in nations, unwilling to defend and secure Western civilization, or the American republic. The Islamist, unlike the American, does not understand that human rights are embedded in the dignity of the human because the human is made in the image of God.

The Muslim man is an inferior man to the Christian due to his ideas; he, through his ideas, has not the virtue, the freedom, or the psychological fitness to compete. The Islamist is the least innovative of man. Unproductive and regressive, his strength lies only in the creation of children and the vehemence of the spleen he vents toward the Westerner.

The American must prepare himself for eventual full-scale war this century or the next with the Islamist. The objective outsider knows the demography of the European and the palsied and timorous nature of the European personality and politics, exacerbated by the fallout of the Second World War; a most substantial increase in Islamic power in this territory of the world must be expected. In the inevitable war between the Islamist and the American which will ring as days of infamy, the American must extirpate the enemy as mercilessly and thoroughly as possible, as this attitude will certainly define the Islamist warrior and his jihad. Such a battle will bear the mentality of the street fight; an outcome much decided by the desire for victory. The American will have to consider his exceptional military tradition, and its members' preference of death to capitulation, and must remember he is the steward of liberty for the world.

The Western cause is enormously unhelped by the welfare programs of the domestic European government, dedicated only to re-election; these programs finance and reward the most pledged opponents of Western existence, enabling this flagitious cabal to cogitate the murder of innocent civilians. The man of this land must refuse to coalesce with the European tradition of multiculturalism, the blueprint of disharmony, and the viaduct for home-grown terrorism, and continue his insistence for the full assimilation of the immigrant that has chosen to make America his new home.

Responsibility for Education

For the American here, the education of his children and adolescence is of the uppermost rank; no other issue

Exceptional America

carries greater weight for him. He carries this burden often with an almost horizontal back, recognizing with great shrewdness that education is the life vest of American exceptionalism and the ultimate buoy of the individual in personal stormy seas. He understands that the responsibility for the education of his child lies with him, not the state.

But the American confronts a crisis; he is at his most encumbered. The elementary and secondary education system of his nation, formerly the most prized of the world, symbolized to the outsider by the yellow school bus, is today but a shadow of its former self. While not yet immediately visible to the outsider, statistical research utilizing various measures and the word of the older generation insists the American child now lags in various educational measurements. It is not only the American suffering this predicament; it is widely and evenly spread throughout the West but the opposite is true for the civilization of the East. Of particular uneasiness are the areas where deficiency is most pronounced: mathematics and science. The strategic survival of any nation depends on science for science and security are inextricably linked; the American need only look to his Israeli friend, a man of unparalleled scientific brilliance. The great threat to the American and the Western civilization which he has dominated is that his and their scientific lead has been significantly closed. The American child is more unlikely than ever to go on and pursue science in the latter years of his secondary education or in his college. The areas crucial in the future of the world, and essential for the challenges of the twenty-first century will benefit the students with the highest levels of mathematics, science and creativity; this must once more become this land's focus.

These are not the only matters of concern that have the American wiping the sweat from his brow; the educators and industry representatives of his schools espouse an altered, vacuous brand of Americanism. In accompaniment of the burgeoning American exceptionalism of the homeschooling experience, the man here, I must say having visited the schools of this man, must reclaim the classrooms of his children; too long the hostage of government intervention and union collaboration. The classroom of the average American school is today the tool of inculcation for the atheistic, politically correct and self-flagellating collectivist. The American flag must remain more visible than the school mascot in the American's schools; she should be suspended in every classroom, gymnasium, lobby and office. The national anthem must continue to be sung at school assemblies and athletic events; these matters of patriotism are central to the greatness of the American nation and any exceptional educational experience. At a secondary level, the American should mandate constitution classes; elementary school should devote a full year to the geography of the United States.

De Tocqueville said of American education:

> Americans are taught from birth that they must overcome life's woes and impediments on their own. Social authority makes them mistrustful and anxious, and they rely upon its power only when they cannot do without it. This first becomes apparent in the schools, where children play by their own rules and punish infractions [which] they define themselves.

Exceptional America

While the illiterate and ignorant have fashioned history of the English-speaking nations in the clothes of their own self-loathing, generations of young British, Australian, and American children leave the doors of their classroom, awash with guilt. The red pens of the elites have ensured that historical exploration now bears the label of genocide, a mere chapter of the broader, vile chronicle of exploitation and racism. The education bureaucrat of this nation urges the imparting of suspicion on the founding principles. This revisionist history that wears on its wrist a black armband endangers a generation of Americans and English-speaking people, to whom the world's liberty will one day be bequeathed. The American child must be pushed to his limit; educational standards must always remain high for nothing rates higher than high school achievement. Schools and universities alike must be prescient in their educational curriculum content; they must always educate students for employment posts that do not yet exist, such is the mark of the true leading nation. The man here must prepare his future generations, with reference to the new world age which he has ushered in, for the likely roles of the future.

To secure his freedom, the American must address with urgency these matters, restoring honesty and pride to the curriculum, and correcting the national narrative in the mind of his young. It will not be until:

- the birthdays of Washington and Lincoln are again celebrated with their symbols of honesty: the cherry tree and the return of change to a customer in New Salem;
- Columbus, and other explorers are presented as the courageous innovators that they were;

- the First Thanksgiving is taught as an event celebrating the friendship of Pilgrims and Indians, through reenactments and a meal;
- Constitutional classes are instituted and required in secondary schools;
- Benjamin Franklin taught as the universal man universally revered that he was;
- Boston Massacre and Boston Tea Party revealed as great and courageous events;
- the poem and story of the midnight ride of Paul Revere is included;
- the Revolution portrayed as the glorious event it truly was;
- John Adams and Thomas Jefferson focused on as Founding Fathers and important Presidents, followed later by Theodore Roosevelt;
- Lewis and Clark are taught as heroes of the Louisiana Purchase;
- manifest Destiny is accepted as reality;
- the great inventions and their inventors, such as the steamboat, telegraph, steel plow, reaper, telephone, phonograph, and assembly line, are taught;
- men such as the father of the Green Revolution, Norman Berlaug, recognized;
- the Civil War taught as the great moral triumph;
- the trinity of constitutional amendments, the thirteenth, fourteenth, and fifteenth, accomplishing the end of slavery;
- the right of women to vote as a natural progression of liberalism;
- the role of America in advancing democracy, particularly in the Spanish-American War and both World Wars, and;

- the work of Alexis de Tocqueville appears in secondary textbooks and studied in depth in later years,

that the American will have truly reclaimed the classrooms of his children. These are the entrepreneurs, inventors and overall stewards of this nation and the world. Further to this, the American child and teenager must be taught to refuse to place any limit on individual human potential, and the role of Western civilization. This nation has led the civilization of the West and it will be the young American of today who will be charged with the responsibility of preserving the greatness and superiority of the West over the Rest. He must study the foundational texts of this civilization: the King James Bible, Isaac Newton's *Principia*, John Locke's *Two Treatises of Government*, Adam Smith's *Moral Sentiments* and *Wealth of Nations*, Edmund Burke's *Reflections on the Revolution in France*, Charles Darwin's *Origin of Species*, and William Shakespeare's plays and selected speeches of Abraham Lincoln, Winston Churchill, and William Wilberforce. The middle-aged American is the most educated, and the most purely educated of his peers, and the same must continue to be said of all proceeding generations for the American to uphold his greatness. Of the real threats posed to the American of today, few can be ranked higher in priority than this. Having journeyed through this great land, I must say, that if the American is to continue his leadership of not only his nation but those of others, he must determine with finality that his children should be neither educated, nor more aptly, indoctrinated, by men with only contempt for his natural state of tradition.

Nick Adams

The puritanical thoughts of the American are often unmatched in action. This nation is not without its shame; its house a sanctuary for the avowed abortionist; the deed of the home tragically protected by the law. No right or matter more bitterly divides the American than that of life; it must be said that this land is also the home of the most valiant supporter of life, a paradox only possible in this nation. The conflict of two fundamental rights that cannot coexist inevitably forces a clear choice, and the American, as the stained pages of history reveal, has erred monstrously in his chosen path. Denied it cannot be: there exists a fundamental right to exercise control over what occurs to one's body. But there exists also the right of the unborn child to live; to life. For the spinal column of social morality to exist, the aircraft carrier in the sea of freedom must always ensure that the rights of one individual end where the rights of another begin. The American must understand the fundamental right to life is his only unlimited right, ultimate and trumping in its nature. When this right is absent, so must liberty be. Without life there can be no future life; without the right to pursue life, the famous Constitution of the American is rendered worthless. He must conduct the deepest of searches of the air, sea and land of his national and personal conscience, realizing the inescapable that abortion is antithetical to his nation in that it denies the dreams of the unborn. It will only be when the American conceives the truth: that his destiny cannot be fulfilled that he gives voice to those that could not, cannot and will not be able to vote or speak. Innocent life must be cherished; without it, innocence is lost in all respects.

In similar fashion, the visitor feels that this land bears in very small parts an almost secular fascism, intent on redefining the greatest and most fundamental institution of civilization. While there success is limited to a handful of havens, many have successfully redefined the institution to permit the marriage of the homosexual; a definition that removes the very need of the institution, and contrary to the moral character of this nation and its commitment to God's best. Sadly some of the Americans have forgotten that the sole reason for this institution in principle was the social regulation for the obligations associated with procreation. This is not to suggest those marriages of man and woman incidentally unable to conceive due to age or infertility are irrelevant; in principle definition, they are included. But marriage of two of the same sex is in principle, impossible, redefining the institution to the point of removing the need. These are matters that the American must deal with, for his full potential to be realized.

Chapter 10

THE FUTURE

> "America will always do the right thing, but only after exhausting all other options."
> Winston Churchill

Many outsiders assert with conviction ringing in their voice, feigning objectivity, the decline of America has begun; the drooped American, low on morale, uncharacteristically consigns himself to ostensible inevitability. But I find that this great nation is not senescent or timeworn; the eagle shows not even the slightest of gray. The profundity of the words of the former President Reagan, the great artisan and shaper of current American prestige; the legacy of who roosts in the modern American, must be recalled to the occasional man here who sits around the kitchen table with slumped shoulders.

> Double—no, triple—our troubles and we'd still be better off than any other people on earth.

The historian suggests the reign of the American took formality with the conclusion of the Second World War and continued with the victory of the Cold War, into the twenty-first century. The events of the last century are irrepressible matters of factuality; the real age of American hegemony an imprecise science. The terrorist attack on this soil in September 2001 awoke him; a sleeping giant awakened from his slumber to find the battle lines of culture drawn. This is a battle the American and men of other lands are, understandably and most rightfully, committed to.

The greatness of this man is in relative infancy; the clock of this country is, not by any stretch I believe, ticking out. The American must retain his confidence, preferably imperiousness; this is the most effective rampart I know available to defend from those forces, domestic and foreign, seeking through temptation the descent of his magnificent nation. The success of the American rolls in on the wheels of his own conviction of his exceptionalism; the removal of this secret ingredient will fell the grand American experiment most spectacularly and expeditiously. This is why the paternity of political correctness, and its offspring of cultural relativism and equality of outcome through capacious government, with their agenda of confidence destabilization, must be rendered barren. If these socialistic theses infest or dilute the values of the man here, bearing him a trembling hand and quivering upper lip, the American will no longer share susceptibility but be the victim of the agenda of his enemies.

A mountain may stand before this man but he, of immense faith, a believer in providence, should know the record of history will reflect exclusively his actions. The accuracy of the prophecy of the sixteenth President of the United States, the man who guided the American through the most devastating experience in his national history, Abraham Lincoln, staggers and ought to be etched in the minds of the men of this country in the small towns and big cities. His words:

> America will never be destroyed from the outside. If we falter and lose our freedoms, it will be because we destroyed ourselves.

The enemy of the American is unlike any of his history; there exists no tangible external enemy of mammoth proportion. The most protuberant of challenges facing the man of this land is ensuring his future befalls not that of the great European civilizations of history; warding off the very ills that felled these once unassailable societies. The continuation of the great experiment of the American and his land is contingent on the unchanging of the laboratory setting and equipment. The same way the hand of the American must not quaver; his hand must also not be numbed by embracing the comforts of retirement; an aversion of risk and becoming reticent to expend energy and resource in defending or spreading his values. He must retain his natural adolescent quality to ensure his nation remains hegemonic. A decline in civic virtue would be most unbecoming of the American, precipitating the drawing of the curtains on the finest show on the greatest stage. The man here must, in his treatment of his enemies, benefit as he did with the conventional enemy of the past. Unity, flexibility, renewal and drive must be the outcomes of the presence of these enemies, and in this way, the American can once more triumph.

The narrative of the American is synchronously compelling, unique and rousing; it is of little surprise the American enters the recruiting stations of his hometown to volunteer for war in great number. This nation has navigated itself to the precipice several times, teetering on the rim of disaster, loss and mediocrity; each time recuperating with velocity to inaugurate a new zenith of exceptionalism and strength through fidelity to values. This should not be lost on the American; with history the basis of the future, only an apostasy of these fixed and enduring values can deprive him his exceptional existence. A new battle was forged at the conclusion of the Second World War, one which the American has sidestepped in large part; greatly assisted by the transformation of his nation in the post-war era to Cold War America, which entrenched its opposition and fear of socialism.

Capital and Capitalism

The grandness of this nation, I discover, lies in her human capital and structural capitalism. The American combines with perpetuation his appetite and dreams, fetching a vision of mammoth proportion. The population of the American providing an abundance of workers is not his sole natural advantage, this becomes clear to me; his extraordinary geographic and geological systems place him in a most enviable position. This land and its man are rich in coal, natural gas and other sources of energy.

The universities of the American, while too frequently contaminated with proponents of Fabianism, remain not simply world-class but world-leading institutions, helping engineer exceptionalism, exceedingly in science, business and informatics. These universities are mostly flushed with financial endowment, a situation greatly unfamiliar to the educational institutions of the outsider's countries, allowing greater emphasis on research and development.

Nick Adams

The age of information that the American dominates has a most diminutive chance of concluding in the near future; this century will continue to allow him to prosper through his ingenuity. The language of the computer is English; the American must continue to ensure all technological code remains thus, as technology is climacteric to the effective control of any modern hegemony. The American must link where possible the college degree to the job, without impinging his freedom or opportunity, to ensure his viability.

The structure of capitalism in the life of the American is exceptional in the incentive it avails for work and innovation. It would appear that the man here is closest to parity between the levels of work and corresponding benefit; his capital gains tax paltry, compared to the outsider. The large populations of this land mean that the economies of this nation are economies of scale. The local focus of the American, with his state-centric calibration, breeds competition between the fifty states, resulting in the best outcome. If one of this land's states offers tax concession within an industry, the other must follow suit or lose industry and employment. Within the American capitalist structure bides an investment proclivity; commensurate with the risk propensity inherent in this man, displaying a glaring belief and faith in people far more profound than the cultures of the outsider. The American is exceptional in his work ethic and makes himself greatly available to his employer. Today the European is either at university or retired; his time in employment most condensed between these two stages.

The once enormous population of this expansive land is today dwarfed by the outside nations of the Pacific region like China and India; circumstances beyond the American's control. Whatever loss this man may incur as a result of the global demography appears to be compensated by his ingenuity, model of government, faith and advancement. The eye of the visiting outsider observes continually the slew of expectant mothers, queue of strollers and classes of young children in the department stores, eateries and book shops of the American. The American, naked of the spiritual morass that bedevils the outsider, replaces almost every death with a birth; a stark contrast to most of his Western cousins. Economic contraction is a natural consequence of demographic decline, further bolstering the case for American optimism. The lure of freedom and opportunity, with the awareness that anyone can be an American, continues to increase the number of Americans. This form of growth would be most problematical for social cohesion in any other nation; not so for the American, who has demonstrated an exceptional ability to fundamentally integrate great swathes of incoming immigrants into his culture, institutions and existing national identity. The specter of sustained growth should remind the man here that he can ill-afford a path of entitlement or expectation of government largesse.

The Admiration of Others

The citizens of the developing world harbor great affinity for the American, and his way of life and seek to emulate him; these are the immotile feelings of the people of nations such as Lithuania, Poland, Eastern Europe, and Africa. Even a silent, growing minority across Latin and America and the Middle East share these desires; oppression removed and the reign of freedom to be restored, particularly the freedom of religious faith. This emerging trend is reported with near silence but should reaffirm the American's values; he should celebrate them, not apologize for them. He must continue to be a refuge for the talented young of the outsider; driven from their nations to his arms for he represents an open door to the walls of their homelands. Becoming American is a notoriously difficult task; the Green Card the most elusive immigration document in the world. The American must make it easier for those that have great affection for and will enrich his society to gain his nationality; importing educated talent in all areas must again become a priority for him. He must be careful to not sully his mental image of immigration with the illegal variety that wreaks havoc on his southwest borders; legal immigration always has and should continue to prolong and intensify American greatness.

The average American cannot possibly grasp his impact on and for human civilization and the wider world. The power he wields in his innovation, capitalism and medical advances make him a staple in the cupboard of the outsider kitchen. The outsider relies on and looks to the American as it can on no other man, even if he is loathe conceding such. This is as the American is exceptional due to his belief economic freedom, individual liberty and wealth creation; should these be removed here in the homeland, then it can hardly be the case that the American is able to continue to bring these virtuous circumstances to the outside world. It is true that the American identity consists of some almost intangible qualities but the one quality that dances on the lips of even the outsider that is most discernibly tangible is that the American equals freedom. The American is not without his faults but this is his greatest redemption. Just as a candle cannot burn without fire, men cannot live without freedom, and it is the American that provides the fire for the candle of freedom. The free man, wherever from he may hail, is American. Freedom is to the American what the chia seed was to the Aztec: his superfood.

The civilization of the West is the greatest civilization of men. The American is its leader; his leadership matching to its requirements; at times nursing and caressing, at others sharp and robust, but always dynamic. The health of the world is delivered by both the figurative and literal medicine of the West; a civilization that has lead with the model systems of law and politics. The American with his peerless international scientific citations has assisted in the dominance of science. The consumer society and work ethic of the Industrial Revolution breathes life within the borders of this nation. But today the breathing is heavy and intermittent; many of the competitive edges of the American and the West blunted by the advances in equivalent areas of the Rest. The release of oxygen from the Western lung is further hampered by the population statistic; the Asian and African vociferous in growth and numbers compared to the North American, European and Australasian. But the American should take heart in the Anglosphere and Western record; a record that verifies population is no guarantee of exceptionalism. The three finest examples are the comparisons of the three pairs of nations: Indonesia and Australia, Singapore and Malaysia, and Hong Kong and mainland China. Contrasting population, the GDP per capita and the UN-awarded Human Development Index (HDI) based on health, standard of living and opportunity, reveals the American-led Anglosphere stands clearly above its Eastern competitors.

Indonesia has a population of 237 million; Australia a population of 23 million, less than one tenth of that of Indonesia. Indonesia's GDP per capita is (USD $4,744), which places it 122nd in the world. Australia's GDP per capita is (USD $40,836), which places it 12th in the world. Indonesia's HDI is 124th. Australia's HDI Ranking is 2nd. Indonesia has been a settled society for five hundred thousand years; Australia a settled Anglosphere society since 1788. The Australian has advanced in leaps and bounds ahead of the non-Anglospheric society of Indonesia, on its doorstep. For a nation of just over two hundred years, the Australian nation has been the engine of growth and a marvel of human kind in its region, leaping far ahead of societies with historical origins going as far back as 500,000 years.

Malaysia has a population of 28,334,000; Singapore, a population of 5,183,700. Malaysia's GDP per capita is $15,385 which places it 47th in the world. Singapore's GDP per capita is $59,936 which places it 3rd in the world. Malaysia's HDI ranking is 61st. Singapore's HDI ranking is 27th. This comparison of Singapore, a former British colony and Muslim Malaysia reveals why until the latter twentieth century, Malaysia was best known for its rubber and tin production. Singapore is the number one financial centre in Asia, with low taxation, free trade, and a vastly superior society compared to that of Malaysia. It must be said that Malaysia has in recent times become a powerhouse of scientific development and has opened its border for trade; progress only realized when its government adopted Western civilization.

China has a population of 1,339,724,852; Hong Kong a mere 7,061,200. China has a GDP per capita of $8,394.00, placing it 91st in the world. Hong Kong has a GDP per capita of $45,736, placing it 10th in the world. China's HDI ranking is 101st in the world. Hong Kong's HDI is 13th in the world. The tiny provincial island of Hong Kong, since the Treaty of Nanking in 1842, followed by the ninety-nine-year lease signed in 1898, has been a capsule of Western civilization in China, becoming an economic juggernaut, with economic development, representative justice, human rights, educational institutions, and a higher life expectancy than China.

A Civilization in Peril

The American today finds his civilization is in peril; his problems financing public debt and the imbalance of his revenue and expenditure are the historical hallmarks of the decline of a superpower. The financial crisis has always featured in the collapse of the civilization; this knowledge keeps the American awake even when he rests his head on his pillow at night. He knows he is encumbered by the worst crisis since his Depression while the alternative civilization flourishes with stunning growth. The more emotional American even sees parallels with the last occasion of the fall of the West; the once great Roman empire. His understanding of tyranny has always been greatly more philosophical than other men; his sovereignty and civic pride steering him to the reality that tyranny as an opinion based on the actions of his political representatives is as detrimental to national morale as that which is actual and violent.

This land would not be the first to succumb to the consequences of the "blessings of civilization" phase of its life; not the least of which is the loss of human liberty, the ultimate failure of success. This is of course, hardly new with many great men having made such observations.

The American cannot be usurped, unless he commits effective suicide by losing his confidence in his exceptional values, his faith, his abilities and his history, thereby entering the current existence of other nations: stasis. The model of this man, I consider, can only be replicated to a certain extent; economic, geographic and cultural differences, assisted by general outside anti-American sentiment, prohibit this. Even in the event that nations do embark on similar initiatives of the American formula and do make progress, the American must ask himself: what true benefit is afforded to any nation, such as China, even if she makes advances to close the gap of the exceptionalism of the Westerner if she does not allow her citizens the right to free thought, genuine political representation and a free press? The success of Western civilization is not just matters of science or technology or work ethic; those matters are only enabled through the Western principles that allow humanity to flourish and innovate. The American must utilize his self-confidence to continually deliver the artisan product; he must take great care in his work and impart on it his own definitive style. He should never settle for second best; his infrastructure must symbolize his exceptionalism. The visiting outsider does note that while the famed American quality in infrastructure and building works is abundant in parts; there are areas in which it has slipped.

The American suffers from resentment, envy, and misunderstanding; circumstances driven by the outsider with diminutive appreciation for the profoundly anti-socialist position he holds, and the unabashed manner in which he conveys it. Confidence in the society of socialistic slant is a trait judged harshly and most unwelcome in the conformist and nervous Western world today. The American must never succumb to the criticism or censure of the outsider with programmed jaundice; these green arrows are aimed direct at the heartbeat of the American: his confidence. The remote control of exceptionalism is powered by the batteries of confidence. The absence or non-function of

Exceptional America

these batteries would level the playing field of the American and the outsider considerably. Edicts of relativism and pluralism, accompanied by refutations of exceptionalism are incompatible with confidence, and therefore must be combated by the American mercilessly. The secular intellectual class, a growing minority within this country, must never have their desires acquiesced, and must continue to be seen as they are: citizens holding an American passport, but never flying on the wings of the American eagle.

A man must believe in his nation state, and see himself such, and not a world citizen, unless he has occasion to quell evil in other corners of the world in the pursuit of human freedom. The American in his daily rigors subscribes to this more so than any other man, much to the chagrin of the outsider led by men who hanker for the world devoid of any clear superpower. The fruition of such desires bears an infinitely greater likelihood than any other nation state overwhelming the American, by force or otherwise, to become the new global power. It is fitting then that it is in the freedom-calloused hands of the American that his fate lies. His quintessence of self-determination will always remain intact. If the American is to continue, he must repel with all the force he can muster the nefarious and collectivist demands made by the outsider of him; demands generated by, at best, poor judgment, and at worst, covetousness.

It is relies upon the formal leadership of a nation to project an image of confidence and self-belief to both its people and those abroad. It must be uncompromising, using any military and economic means available to it, to achieve the objectives and best interests of the people by which it has been elected. The American must be vigilant in ensuring that his government and her representatives reflect the intensely anti-socialistic, robustly individualistic and deeply

Christian nature of the nation. While he is safeguarded by the transcendental nature of his nation and culture; the idea that it is America suffers, at least, temporary impurity, each occasion the federal government or White House brings forth policy or takes action more befitting a European nation than fashioned on the visions of the Founding Fathers. The American must avoid any form of cultural totalitarianism for it is this, I feel as I observe his country in operation in large urban centers, which inevitably leads to the mandatory conformity of conduct and thought.

The penetrating Christian faith, philanthropy, charity and commitment to freedom that the American exhales with each breath are testament to his inherent goodness. The French philosopher, de Tocqueville, put it most poignantly:

> America is great because America is good. If America ceases to be good, America will cease to be great.

It must be said that these virtues are so woven in the American blanket that an almost inconceivable departure from them would so powerfully alter the culture; the complete destruction of the nation would not be unlikely.

Exceptionalism is a cyclical mechanism; the exceptional culture is the creator of the exceptional country which in turn is the breeder of the exceptional people. Buoyant, bold, and rewarding, the culture of the American is truly a sight to behold. The American must preserve this liquid of exceptionalism and guard the strength of each of its ingredients. He must remember that no expiration date exists for the idea that is of fundamental truth and sound. Dilution is the weapon and objective of choice for the anti-American; his ammunition the poisonous bullets of political correctness, relativism, pluralism, bureaucratic internationalism all pegs to and under the high-pitched tent of big government. The American must always remember why he has enjoyed great blessing; Israel's interest is theologically important.

Time to Take a Stand

Where this man finds himself right now, I believe to be, not his permanent address, unless he allows it to be. In the life of every nation, no matter how inestimable their power or exceptional their people, exist seasons not of harvest. But it is in these times the American must call upon his Christian decree, embedded in his makeup; if the American believes God to be in control, directing his steps, then he must believe he is exactly where he is supposed to be. The American must in these times believe a hedge of protection surrounds him; that no feat or objective amid these great storms is beyond him. It is this heavy faith that will carry the American forward in his darkest hours and precisely this that sets him apart from any enemy, irrespective of magnitude or firepower. The man who dismisses the American is either most foolish or willfully blind; the tenacity of the American, imbued with biblical belief, cannot be matched.

The American has enormous reason for optimism; his strengths have greater resonance in the world of today and the future than ever before, equipping him to deal with the challenges of the new century. He must be aware that it is only the West that he leads and has fashioned dramatically that can engender in the members of any polity, irrespective of size or location, the greatest potential for individual human creativity. Only those institutions—social, economic and political—conceived by the Western bloodline ensure the best available context for human achievement in the most challenging of circumstances.

He must recall the energetic elasticity and relentless optimism that has seen him remain ahead in the face of disruption and disappointment and remember his exceptional military tradition. He must remind himself of the improbable experiment of his nation, of his nation's unique narrative; that he is neither ordinary nor average. The American will only fold when he parts himself from spirituality and no longer believes he cannot be uprooted or toppled. It seems to the outsider that the American is prepared to accept finite disappointment but never loses infinite hope. His lexicon is full of words of optimism such as faith, hope, belief and victory; and so it must stay if he is to remain the greatest of men. He should find the solace in the words of the Texas Ranger: "No man in the wrong can stand up against a fellow that's in the right and keeps on a-comin'." The American is a man in the right, with resilience that sees him fall down seven times, but get up eight. He must continue in his proud tradition and find an answer to every problem and not see a problem for every answer; the latter the more common cause for the pessimist, mostly found in the socialistic nations.

As the SEAL finds comfort in the twenty-third psalm of the Bible, so must the average man here. Hope must continue to grow deep in the bones of the American, thriving in every inch of him. He must continue to see life as a leap of faith, a bold declaration of hope. He must continue to give meaning to life from the frontline, not wait from the sideline for life to provide him such. The American does not find himself; he creates himself. From the Navy SEAL to the New York Firefighter to the Texas Ranger, each American has within them an exceptional patriotism, a belief in Providence, a love of the military, a devotion to freedom, and a disposition to bravery.

The American must stay the course; he must remain devoted to the visions of his founders and their documents, and continue to be the bastion of optimism, freedom, individualism and Christianity for the preservation of not just himself, but humanity in total. He must retain his faith-based consciousness, and must carry it with him in all the arenas of life. Only he can secure Western civilization and the American republic.

Chapter 11

THE NATURE OF THE AMERICAN BOOMERANG

Even in the calendar of pronounced sun set days of American dominance, the visitor cannot divorce himself of the contagious optimism or inspiration embodied by the people scattered right through the nation. He cannot help but feel that the seed of individual brilliance and creativity that so animates the individual spirit of the American will again burst forth and flower into something greater and more powerful than anything the world has yet seen. Even if the vitreous case, comprising almost exclusively glass materials, of American decline is accepted, then such a case must only apply in the collective sense. The individual American is certainly not in decline. This nation bears an almost plethoric number of individuals relentless in their pursuit and attainment of success; even if in benign decline collectively, the outsider cannot part himself of the view that this nation is at any time but a heartbeat away from a rebirth or renaissance. It was once observed by historian Henry Adams that the minds of the earliest American settlers operated as "a mere cutting instrument, practical, economical, sharp, and direct"; the outsider finds little evidence in contemporary America of a blunted mind; in fact, he could only draw the conclusion that the American mind remains the exceptional instrument of humankind. The outside friend of the American feels a reawakening distinctly possible if the people of America, in addition to their individual effort, once more strive for a major accomplishment as a collective. An innovative national achievement of which every American feels a part would most certainly surge a people and silence the critics.

The American possesses a distinctly bold boomerang nature; carrying the characteristics of the Australian flying tool, he often embarks on a trajectory that travels him far from his origin, but always returns him to his founding position. Both boomerang and American are pioneer tools of self-determination, uniquely crafted in varying materials and size with an adventurous character, and free will. As each part the hands of their respective founders, each is exposed to dangerous temptation and external force, often momentarily accommodating them, straying far from their anticipated course. But both, under the watchful guide of the eagle and Creator of all things, and something intrinsic within their making, unfailingly returns them to their rightful place.

The boomerang is unlike the ball; it is true that the ball enjoys good bounce, but it is a matter of science that the each successive bounce is lower than the previous. The boomerang suffers no such ailment, returning in the identical condition with which she began her journey.

The American has a difficult return journey, considering his navigation takes place in these hours of severely limited light, but as his past demonstrates, he has the supernatural increase that not even the finest boomerang can offer. The American invariably returns from the adverse journey in greater advance and condition than that which he departed.

This return journey must be travelled in the same space or vehicle that all other travel has occurred. It is often asserted in good faith by the well-meaning, successful American that his people would be well aided by orienting and realigning himself to the outside world; that the answers to America's future lie in an entirely different approach. While it is true that updating and refreshing of his famed formula is not negotiable in meeting the challenges of change in the future, such action must not occur with global eyesight or a marked change in his politics or values. This is a time when the American can ill afford to be convinced that he must temper his values and reach a middle ground, deserting his passion; a message spread by those feverishly practicing the dark arts of spin, an alchemy that can transform a strong but divided society to a weak and synthetic polity. Government activism in areas such as education, research and development and infrastructure would constitute major departures; these are not American answers, although they are delivered with American accents. The return journey of the American is always an American one; noted in the famous words of one President:

> There is nothing wrong with America that cannot be cured by what is right with America.

The visitor to the shores of America is powerfully inspired by what he bears witness to, but gravely frets at that which he has seen lost. He who considers himself a friend of the American would implore him to stay with Reagan and stand with the founders of his nation, in embracing and promoting the value of the individual and the exceptionalism of the American experiment. The American must be jolted out of complacency; stirred up and finding no satisfaction in past glories, he will be at his optimum. He must rise up with boldness, perpetuating his dedication to the manifesto of freedom and patriotism. The visitor is optimistic for the American; not least because of his ability to mobilize in great number to effect change and his profound belief in the power of his ballot. His clamor for self-improvement of calls forth a reciprocal faithfulness for the state of his nation, the disdain for docility deep. The virtues of freedom, liberty and opportunity are the branches of the exceptional tree bearing the fruit of the spirit: self-control, goodness, love, joy, patience and kindness. History reveals the uncanny propensity of the American to retain or revert, whatever the call of the hour. Vigilance has always been the great need of the American hour, and so it is once more. The synergism of faith, patriotism, individualism, and military will always reopen the door to the stairway upward. The American boomerang still bears the fingerprints of the Cold War; it imprinted on him the value of change in direction.

The resourcefulness of the American has weakened him for he has leveled his playing field to great degree in business but this is, I do not consider, problematic; he belongs to such a nation that his competitive edge will almost always exist save for his own intervention.

Common Cultures, Shared Values

The American would do well to continue to align himself with his natural partner; his cousins of the English-speaking world, known to many as the Anglosphere. These men share a passion for democracy and capitalist, free-market economies. They are bound to the American in common literature and history, the rule of law, traditions of constitutional government, individual liberty, and the right to life, liberty and property; language, law, habit and custom are their strings. Their fight has seen them battle together from the beaches of Normandy to the sands of Iraq. The Anglosphere, similar to its American leader, has a distinctly American disposition, open and undefined by blood or ancestry but by common and shared values. As the American boomerang hurtles through his journey back to the Promised Land, these nations are the wind in his back, and always in the American backpack. In matters of foreign entanglement, nations must be allies, not clients of the most benign power of our lifetime, the American. It is only the nations of the West that have bred liberty in the hearts and minds of men; they must continue to be embraced. Just as the greatest threats to Western civilization are not outside civilizations, the greatest threat to the American nation is the American people.

The friend of the American, spurred to speak out of turn in the face of the duplicity of the American elites, and the potential ramifications of their words and actions if heeded, feels the need to remind him that freedom would have long ago shriveled and republican democracy waned in the other countries of the world, were it not for him. For as long as this nation stands, it is clear that this world will have and continue to have a model of freedom and exception; a target at which to aim and a level of which to aspire. The American must not only remember but affirm his story past. Existing in the ether of the outside world is the silent majority of the outsider that believes the future of world history is dependent on the future of this glorious nation. Such a visitor can only implore and beseech the American, as he moves into the twenty-first century, to reaffirm the values that have carried his brave experiment and delivered his breathtaking exceptionalism. These values continue to shape not only America but the world, for decades and generations to come. Ronald Reagan, that great defender of American exceptionalism and global improvement, once told the American:

> Freedom is never more than one generation away from extinction. We didn't pass it to our children in the bloodstream. It must be fought for, protected, and handed on for them to do the same, or one day we will spend our sunset years telling our children and our children's children what it was once like in the United States where men were free.

The American must never supplant his own ambition for the ambitions of the state; obedience is the termite that slowly feeds on the structural foundations, destroying its existence while preserving deceptively its outside. It is also the termite that will infest the American boomerang and take away its flight permanently. The American must continue to see that individualism is the foundation of American society. The American appears to instill in his young a distaste for submission to authority. This must continue for the prosperity of this nation.

The Battle Has Just Begun

It is now more than ever; with the enemies lining at the gates, and world sentiment convinced that the American experiment has finally expired, that the American remember the words of Ronald Reagan, and call on the official final words of the Navy SEAL:

> We train for war and we fight to win. I stand ready to bring the full spectrum of combat power to bear in order to achieve my mission and the goals established by my country. The execution of my duties will be swift and violent when required, yet guided by the very principles I serve to defend.
>
> Brave men have fought and died building the proud tradition and feared reputation that I am bound to uphold. In the worst of conditions, the legacy of my teammates steadies my resolve and silently guides my every deed. I will not fail.

The American must win the battle that lies before him. The man of every other nation depends on him. With steely resolve and fierce determination, he must remember who he is, where he comes from, and all that has occurred in his history. He must continue to breathe liberty; should he ever gasp for breath, he must inhale from his reliable source of freedom to once more regain his creativity, desire, and exceptional brilliance. He must know in his heart and mind that men of every color, creed, and denomination depend on him and his country's ideas as oxygen.

The conservative American is the man who delivered American exceptionalism. He is also the man upon whose future America weighs. Greatness is never awarded; it is always earned. He earns it with the fire and fight in his heart—the qualities that set the extraordinary man apart from the ordinary. All any man of the slightest intellect can do—and must do—is thank God for this nation and the true Americans that uphold her values.